Wordpress

How to Build a Wordpress Website on Your Own Domain From Scratch

(Best Wordpress Plugins for Developing Amazing and Profitable)

Walter Dobbs

Published By **Tyson Maxwell**

Walter Dobbs

Wordpress : How to Build a Wordpress Website on Your Own Domain From Scratch (Best Wordpress Plugins for Developing Amazing and Profitable)

ISBN   978-1-77485-681-9

No part of this guidebook shall be reproduced in any form without permission in writing from the publisher except in the case of brief quotations embodied in critical articles or reviews.

Legal & Disclaimer

The information contained in this ebook is not designed to replace or take the place of any form of medicine or professional medical advice. The information in this ebook has been provided for educational & entertainment purposes only.

The information contained in this book has been compiled from sources deemed reliable, and it is accurate to the best of the Author's knowledge; however, the Author cannot guarantee its accuracy and validity and cannot be held liable for any errors or omissions. Changes are periodically made to this book. You must consult your doctor or get professional medical advice before using any of the suggested remedies, techniques, or information in this book.

TABLE OF CONTENTS

Introduction

You probably frequent a few websites each daily, no matter if it's you're there for entertainment, business or for training. But, have you ever wondered how these sites actually function? What is their structure? What is the way that browsers, computers and cell phones communicate to the web? What are the skills required in the creation of a website? With more than 1 billion websites now available on the web the answers to these questions could be the first step towards understanding the web and developing a new set of skills for the internet.

If you want to create your site successful it is essential to start at the top stage you can locate. It's a bit difficult because there are so many options available for creating your brand new website, it could be difficult to decide which stage to select.

Although there's no perfect stage, WordPress comes extremely close. It's extremely adaptable to an array of web-based sites, from basic websites to explosive internet-based corporate customer-facing facades. The benefits from using WordPress are numerous and they're surprisingly simple to start.

In this guide we'll introduce you with WordPress and provide a clear understanding of the purpose behind it. We'll go through a part of the experiences it offers and outline the major benefits of choosing the platform for your website. It is best to start with the basics

Chapter 1: Introduction To Website

What is the purpose of a website?

A website is a collection of interlinked, freely accessible Web pages which share the same domain name. Sites may be developed and maintained by a person, group organizations, businesses or even a company to satisfy a range of requirements. Together, all free websites form the World Wide Web.

Despite the fact that it's occasionally the past known as "web page" it's not true because a website is comprised of several pages on a website. A website is also known as"web presence, "web site" or simply "website".

Here are the eight distinct kinds of websites:

1. Landing pages The landing page is the main focal point of your website and is the foundation of a brand. The landing page is the place where users navigate through different sections of your site as well as be used as a channel for conversion. Since many visitors arrive at your page's landing area, it is where the layout is the most crucial factor.

A landing page could be built different forms, but when planning, it is essential to consider the reason of the landing page, as the primary route and primary destination for site visitors. Define the purpose of the business and provide the compelling incentive clearly. Create the layout and pecking order on the page that leads to the landing page. Utilize your image's color range, logo and images that are relevant to your business. The landing page sets the mood for your image of the business, therefore it should tell a story about your company's identity through images and text.

2. Magazine websites magazines have photos, articles and videos that are informative and educational. In the last two decades, the business of magazines has changed from a print-only platform to an excellent digital layout. The magazine site type function excellently for educational sites particularly distributions from associations and colleges.

If you're thinking about creating your magazine website, begin by creating a system. Your visitors should be able to see a similar design no matter when they arrive on the page that they are on, and every article should be in the same format and layout. Keep in mind how responsive your general design is to different sizes of screens to ensure that your content is easily readable for both desktops and mobile phones.

3. Web-based business sites: A website -based business website is an online shopping platform where customers can purchase items as well as services through your company. A well-designed web-based site for business allows users to easily browse products, browse channels by categories, highlight the best deals , and even make sales.

4. Blogs include regularly updated articles, photos and videos. Blogs started out with less formal individual content that was compared to magazines. But from then onward, the lines between them have blurred, and today it's extremely common for major businesses and brands to own a blog. The addition of master content enhances the overall credibility of an organization or individual. Blogs can also be used to create content for social media and emails campaigns.

In the event that a blog is not maintained, it isn't the only thing that can be problematic for small businesses. You should have a team and procedure in place to make sure that the content is up-to-date before you consider launching one. It's much better to create a blog, but instead provide a few videos and tutorials, rather as opposed to having an outdated blog.

5. Portfolio websites Portfolio sites give creative professionals a platform to showcase their work. This is perfect for experts as well as scholars, planners and furniture makers, as well as producers and many more.

When you build an portfolio, there's not a justification to list every single project you've worked on. In the end, focus on forming categories of things and including the most impressive work in each category. Portfolio websites are more imaginative, and this is the ideal place to try out unique styles and add interesting highlights.

6. Points of Arrival Points or arrival refers to a page layout designed to promote an event which encourages guests to take a specific action.

The information you present on a page should be kept to a minimum and should highlight what call to action (CTA) you'd like your client to follow. Allow plenty of empty space in the vicinity of your CTA and leave out any elements that aren't associated with the reason to accomplish that goal for other pages.

7. Media sites on the internet there are around 2.77 billion users on the online media and there are a myriad of platforms available. No matter who your audience is, you'll probably find these people in Facebook and Twitter and Instagram and Snapchat as well as LinkedIn. Although you aren't able to alter the actual platforms, you have some influence in the appearance of your site and the content that is driving share of media on the internet.

Make sure you have a consistent view of all your media websites and websites, so that visitors immediately recognize that your image is at the bottom of your page. Use a similar logo and shade choices. Select a character or voice that shines throughout the entire substance.

When creating content, think on items with a good chance of being shared online via media, such as engaging photos, infographics, videos deep-dive reports, and deals for free.

8. Contact pages and catalogs Contact pages or a directory page allows customers to contact you or other people. This kind of website works well when you want to display a list of people or companies within an organization. For example, a nearby cafe directory lists nearby eateries with menus, price ranges phone numbers, and audits.

The concept of an association is to provide an opportunity to create the creation of a directory website. For instance, a connection of dentists within a city could include every aspect of their expertise, as well as their contact information. Make sure to keep this option in your pocket to hand out to clients. Through boards, print magazines, and paper for instance , you can discover customers through a variety of ways, each challenging to help them come to a profit. Openness online, such as the pay-per-snap system or show promoting, for instance, allows you to select how broad and how thin your openings are.

Top Five Benefits of a Great Web Site

Brand Exposure, as well as support

Customers are introduced to brands from a variety of perspectives. Customized showcasing via bulletins, prints magazine, radio and other media for example - expose customers in a variety of ways, each challenging to help them come to an understanding with a revenue. Online openness, like pay-per-snap and show-promoting, for instance, allow you to decide how wide and/or limited your accessibility is. Frameworks like Facebook's Ad stage as well as Google AdWords (Google Ads) allow for an extremely active brands that are focusing even down to postal codes or even a customer segment.

Your website at this point can help your brand image by offering an important, valuable and important information. This can be a way to make a point of a later commitment to purchase products or services, as well as the possibility of references from the viewer. Think about this as a "do great" chance. When you're asked, what you're getting for testing at Costco or Safeway? In the event that they draw you in and providing something significant to experience in return, they are able to sell more of that "thing". If you're a circuit tester , offer suggestions on how to arrange new tasks or a piano instructor can make a video about an "starter" exercise Brewers can offer an opportunity to visit the distillery. If you can make something that is important to those who come across your work, you'll be able to make more of them "yours".

Engaging with Clients or Customers

When you provide your clients with contact points with access to numbers or messages, or even social networks - you're offering a means to your clients or likely clients to come into your company. For inquiries and to assess leads or purchases.

Client Education

What better way to inform your customers on your product or service? Your website's content could be tailored to possible goals, and provide specific information that supports the decision of your client to purchase your product or service.

Reputation Management

Reputation Management was an 'offline practice in past times. Reputation management in 2017 must be reliable and organized.

Conversion

72% of people who performed an internet search for local businesses were in a store within 5 miles. In providing all the details necessary to make an option to buy and recommending easy way to finish the exchange - you'll be able to make sure you are able to get a slice of that purchase. More than a five-mile drive, you could - by exerting a small amount of effort take on those businesses yourself!

What is the purpose of a Web-based Website?

Different kinds of websites have different purposes, based on who the intended audience is.

Some sites are geared to sell products, while other websites are designed to provide useful information, while others are primarily for entertainment. Let's look at one of the many types of websites on the market.

* The Purpose of Informative/Practical Information Websites: The motivation behind a data driven site is to pass on explicit, supportive data to a particular client/crowd so the readers discover some new information or comprehend a point better. The sites are designed around significant information. They may include "how to's" as well as tricks and tricks fixes and repairs directions, information about support such as headings, guidelines and more.

*The Purpose of Entertainment Websites: These websites provide entertaining information for visitors. Online magazines, tattle based sites, news of big names and sports integration films, human expressions as well as diverting websites and so on. These websites are designed to be easy to browse and frequently updated to keep visitors coming back to get more information. They are able to be more engaging using dynamic material such as recordings of slideshows, digital broadcasts and more.

* The purpose of E-Commerce Websites: The main reason behind web-based websites for businesses is to provide goods to customers. The most effective websites are meticulously developed to ensure a higher number of purchases. To be successful, businesses must include the entire range of modern shutting techniques and upsell techniques that have been proven to improve the probability that guests will purchase. There are a variety of important components that make up an effective business website, including getting rid of grating during the purchasing process and making the checkout simple and easy while also making the site fast and appealing, upselling customers on related items and thereby increasing sales, decreasing the time it takes to return a truck, encouraging customers who have purchased before to buy and again, remarketing customers who haven't yet purchased using the right payment options, using an adaptable plan of action and so on and on.

* The goal of Service-Based websites for businesses: the idea behind an assistance-based business website is to convince users to become customers of the company. This is achieved by positioning the company as a reliable expert, trustworthy, and reputable specialist cooperative in the market. The customers will be able to pre-screen potential specialists by exploring their websites before settling on a phone call. In this conversation they will try to find the most suitable company that can meet their specific requirements. They want to know the level of mastery that the company has and the type of work they can expect whatever the company is in good standing and the length of time it has been in operation for. Visitors could benefit from external input through the sharing of documents and information that show your expertise, a visual layout that demonstrates your efforts, audio recordings and client testimonials, for example.

* The purpose behind Blogs The reason behind blogs is to offer an regularly refreshed website or page, usually that is run by a single person or

small gathering published in casual or informal style. Websites can be created efficiently on the internet using various free applications, like, wordpress.com. There are a variety of personal and professional journals online out there to read and provide insight into the daily life of an individual. Websites can be used for diversion reasons or as a diary on the internet or used by companies to keep their customers with what's going on. The advantage of blogs is that it is easy for a novice to keep track of almost nothing but the most basic information.

*The Purpose social media websites: The primary reason for the existence of online media websites is to facilitate to share information and interact with family members, friends and friends, colleagues, associates as well as strangers. Media sites on the web make quick and easy work the process of creating an organization of groups to keep in touch with each other, and to share daily experiences, photos, interests as well as inclinations and more. Informal groups are useful for commercial and personal reasons. Companies make use of informal networks to establish close relationships with their customers that allow them to receive feedback on their products as well as benefits, and also allows them to learn the needs of their customers and desire.

What do you require to create an online presence?

Find a domain name The first step to developing your site is to choose the way you'll have it hosted. There are a variety of options to consider. For instance, you could simply create a blog on a free sub-domain using WordPress.com or you could have an self-hosted site with the real domain name and not just a sub-domain. It's probably better to use an actual domain name (and not an unrelated sub-domain). While a sub-domain for free isn't always the best option especially when you require credibility with a polished and professional appearance, as well as an impressive mark for your website and business.

Create a domain email address Another benefit of using an individual domain name is the ability to create customized emails for domains (i.e.

you@yourdomain.com). A custom domain email address can increase the credibility and demonstrates the expertise your website requires. Many people won't have the desire to collaborate with a company that doesn't have an email address for its domain.

Choose a website building application or platform: When you've decided on a domain, it's a great time to think about your website. There are a variety of site building platforms and applications for download. While some people prefer to build a website with no preparation, and others use WordPress however, many others are inclined towards the simplicity and ease of use offered by simpler web design. There are numerous simplified web designers in the market and it's hard to pinpoint which is the most impressive. Each has each its own unique set of advantages and drawbacks, they all accomplish the same thing. They allow anyone, from beginners to designers, to design an entire website using an easy-to-use supervisor, with no programming expertise or knowledge needed. Some of the simpler web designers that are available are Wix, Website.com, Weebly and Squarespace.

Design and alter your website using a plan layout It's not an enjoyable feeling to gaze at a blank white page, and not knowing what to do next. This is why the majority of web designers have a library of web composition templates to use as a starting point. Web composition layouts are an already-designed web composition that allows you to create an appealing and professional looking website without the necessity of hiring an expert in web design and also without the requirement of any programming or knowledge of configuration.

It is important to note that not all layouts are the same. Certain layouts are basic that offer only the basics and others are massive displays with lavish extras. In general, the formats are created for specific kinds of locations and ventures, such as eating establishments and online journal. Once you've selected an appropriate format and best page layouts are in place, you can begin tweaking the layout - you are able to modify the website's shading plan and textual style, the foundation of the page and more. These are all done by the administrator and there aren't any codes to modify or write. Some web designers allow you alter the layout at levels of code, but it is not necessary to have any specific level of expertise and knowledge to accomplish this.

Use visual components (logos and images) using visual elements is an effective way to improve the user experience of your site and increase conversion rates, as well as assist in marking your site and increase the attractiveness of your site. The absence of a logo can make your website boring and uninteresting. But, like any other aspect of a website the use of images should be handled with care and consideration. The best practice is to utilize high-quality attractive and interesting images. In terms of a logo design there are a variety different ways to design an appealing logo for your company and website. You could hire a visual designer, or use an online logo maker or can even create one your self. If you plan to use images on your website you must use excellent photography and illustrations. Images that are flimsy and fake images can ruin even the most well-designed website, and will negatively affect the way your visitors think about your site as well as your company. The best option is to hire a photographer artist to create images to use on your site. If you've got the chance and ability to produce the image you're seeking quickly then why not? If you're on a budget plan or even photography, stock images are an alternative that is incredibly effective. There is an abundance of skilled excellent stock photos on the Internet whether paid or free.

For example,

Unsplash - a free

Pixabay - free

Shutterstock.com - paid

GettyImages.com - paid

Dreamstime - paid

If you have a website hosting account, now that you've created your website and have it up and running, now is the perfect time to put it on the Internet to allow people to view it on their devices. Web has is a co-operative that lets you store your website in their server. When users visit your website through the Internet the browser will load the content of your site. There are many kinds of web hosting, and the one you choose depends on the level of security you want, the amount of people who come to your website as well as other factors generally sharing hosting is the most suitable option to start with. and in addition to the fact that it's cost-effective, it's also easy to monitor as everything the technical aspects are handled by the expert co-operative. If you're using a web design company like Wix or Website.com it is not necessary worry about hosting your website as it is provided and managed by the expert web designer co-op.

Register with Google Analytics: Google Analytics is a web-based investigation tool which lets you observe the way your visitors are cooperating with your website. In particular, you will find out how many people have visited your website, the time they go to your website and which pages were most frequently visited, from which location did they visit your website and much more. All of this information will aid you in understanding your customers better, and identify the areas or pages of your site you'll need to enhance. Most web designers support Google Analytics. It is easy to create the Google Analytics record and then change the following ID created by Google on your web designer's control board. Be aware that certain web designers come with an underlying web insights instrument. If you prefer not to utilize Google Analytics then you should utilize the web insights instrument , with all other things identical.

Setup PayPal When you are selling products or services, or in the event that you require to accept gifts on your website You will need an method to collect installment information. PayPal is an amazing installment solution for allowing payments.

How do you market a new website?

Here are 8 unique ways to help promote your new website:

1. Email Marketing

The success of email marketing is dependent on the development of your contacts list, segmenting it to appeal to different groups of customers. You should also provide important content to encourage users to stay engaged. Always connect to your website as an email source of inspiration and encourage re-visits to your website by sending regularly updated content.

2. Signature for an Individual Email

It is possible to add a link with your website's landing pages, or the specific point to which that you must advance. If the connection connects to your website, make sure that it functions as an actual landing page.

3. Improvements to the site

Understanding how to improve your site's performance in SEO can help boost the natural index of your website. Yet, SEO can be an uneasy process that includes making your website more keyword-friendly and providing quality content and increasing the quality of connections to your website. Through improving SEO, your website will appear near the top of search items for your keywords.

4. Pay-Per-Click advertisements

What's PPC? Pay-per-click ads are paid for to appear on the web crawlers. The most popular paid ads are made through Google AdWords. It is possible to tell Google your budget and then pay when someone clicks your advertisement. This is known as pay-per-click advertising. Make sure that your advertisement is connected to a destination that is identical to the one in the advertisement.

5. Web-based Media

Web-based media platforms such as Facebook or Twitter (with 1 billion users each) are a fantastic way to increase the visibility of your site and improve your blog in the event that your site has one. Include links to your blog, landing page or other web pages (contingent to the notion of the content) within your online media profiles and posts. If you are using social media to promote your website or image, it is essential to understand your target audience. Look for patterns, and use the most popular features across all platforms such as Instagram stories as well as Instagram promotions.

6. YouTube

More than 1 billion users utilize YouTube frequently. This fact, along by the immense popularity of videos is what is what makes YouTube an effective tool to promote your website. Be sure to include an in your video, with a link to your site and provide viewers with a legitimate reason to visit your site.

7. Visitor Blogging

Make sure you differentiate driving websites from your niche and then offer to create websites for visitors to them. Be sure to include an affiliation to your site to the blog post such as in your profile at the end of the article. If you don't consider yourself as a remarkable writer or you're just beginning in the field of content promotion it's essential to acquire the ability to master a few fundamental concepts.

8. Retargeting

If shopping at Walmart online you might see ads for the products you purchased, or similar Walmart items, on other websites. Retargeting is the method used to achieve this an innovation based on treats that embeds a unique code into your website. When guests visit your website the code adds an extra treat to the guest's program. It is possible to display promotions on your website on various sites on the internet, increasing the visibility of your site and the services and products that you require.

Chapter 2: E-Commerce Website

What is an e-commerce site?

The term "web-based" business" or electronic trade refers to a course of action which includes transactions trades that are conducted via the internet. The majority of shopping website - big or small - uses this structure. Any site where you are able to find items to be bought online is considered to be an online business website.

eBay and Amazon the granddads of business online have been redesigned to be an updated and more efficient way of shopping. They're not too old to be considered granddads. However, a higher level of respect is portrayed in the marketplace. Evidently, buying and selling was at this moment a thing in the past however, with the advent the advent of these companies, a websites for business have turned into a much simpler and popular choice for a lot of customers.

People were extremely cautious of these stores to purchase items because they're prone to fraudulent activities and erroneous plans. This is evident to this day but engineers devise solutions to enhance the customer experience. Examples of these arrangements include surveys, exchanges of goods and cash down. These highlights aid customers in making a decision about whether they should purchase items from a business's online website or not.

One of the most obvious differences between an online business site and a traditional website for a business or an organization is in the pillars it encapsulates. A business site can contain information about the company's products and services, so customers must contact the company quickly in case they require assistance from them. A business site functions in a similar way to the way a physical store operates. Customers can purchase items like mastermind conveyance or installments on the same site, without the requirement to contact an individual who can assist customers with their requests. When you start to figure out how to create web-based content for your business will be apparent that it's slightly more difficult to establish an online store in comparison to an ordinary site because of the features and planning elements that the latter demands.

What are the different kinds of eCommerce strategies?

The first step to start your online business is to understand the different eCommerce plans of execution. In general, eCommerce businesses are classified as one of the four categories.

1. Business-to-business (B2B)

The model of business-to-business eCommerce is structured exactly as it is. It's where businesses offer products to various businesses. Different kinds of products incorporate what improves the strategic strategies of another company.

Perhaps the most effective illustration of an B2B company is a product company. Think Salesforce, HubSpot, or SurveyMonkey. These tools are meant to assist the business however it won't look good for the average mother and pop shopper to put money into the big business of programming.

2. Business-to-customer (B2C)

The model of business-to-customer eCommerce is also evident. It's the time when the business can sell its products via the internet or through the phone, directly to buyers.

Business-to-purchaser eCommerce organizations are organizations that you and I visit online consistently to buy things like attire, books, cosmetics, and so on

The top B2C eCommerce firms include giants such as Amazon, eBay, and Alibaba.

It's also essential to keep in mind that B2C businesses don't have to operate solely online as Amazon or eBay.

B2C companies can also have an actual store, and in the event it goes well, could launch an eCommerce website. Some examples of this are huge retail stores that are trendy like Nordstrom, J. Group and H&M And that's just the tip of an Iceberg.

3. Buyer to-shopper (C2C)

A buyer-to-shopper course of action is where one buyer purchases and then offers an item to a different client.

One buyer could use an online platform such as Amazon, Etsy, or eBay to provide products to a different customer. With online eCommerce platforms such as WooCommerce, customers may even create C2C stores on their own. C2C shop on their personal website.

4. Business to business (C2B)

The most popular eCommerce strategy is the purchaser-to-business. This is when the buyer, or a business-minded person, sells services or products to businesses.

Real examples of C2B businesses would be business advisor, an independent graphic architect or an online media influencer who has an immense audience.

What are the various kinds of eCommerce websites?

No matter what eCommerce method you choose each one of them does the things the same way.

Each of the eCommerce stores are run through the internet. That means you'll need the site.

Below are the different kinds of eCommerce sites you should be aware of.

1. Single brand site

A personal brand website is a site that solely sells the products or services of a single person or business. It's also the most acknowledged type of site for those who are starting their own eCommerce shop, as well as is likely the kind of website that you'll start. It doesn't matter which eCommerce strategy you're using. If you're planning for selling your own goods then you'll have to put together an explicit seller site.

For example, if someone visits the B2B Salesforce website it will only show Salesforce products. In the same way, my company is an C2C company. I provide composing aides from independent authors and other items to other freelance essayists. I designed a single website that meets my eCommerce requirements.

2. Online stores

The next kind of eCommerce site is similarly common and is particularly popular for large retailers. Online retailers are larger shops that frequently offer discounts to products from other brands.

For example, Dick's Sporting Goods is where you can purchase a variety of types of outdoor gear and outdoor clothing from different brands. What if we stick to Patagonia? Patagonia model, but adapt this to an internet-based retailer scenario.

If I visit on the Dick's Sporting Goods site, I will be able to set my channels to find Patagonia products. Dick's Sporting Goods doesn't make Patagonia products. The purchasers of the brand purchase massive quantities of Patagonia products directly from Patagonia and then sell them at the higher price of retail on the website. Also, you'll notice it's true that Patagonia isn't the sole name Dick's Sporting Goods sells on its website. Customers can also buy items from competing brands like Columbia, NorthFace, and Nike.

3. Sites of our partners

Retail isn't the ideal method of generating money with an eCommerce site that sells other brands' products. Another option is to create an offshoot website. A member website is where someone sells items from other brands on their website in exchange to a commission.

If you create an online site that generates huge profits the setting up of an online member site is an excellent way to earn extra money.

4. Commercial centers

Another type form of eCommerce site is commercial centers. Commercial centers are an online marketplace where single business owners can showcase their products that can be bought. The most well-known models include Amazon as well as Etsy. Etsy and Amazon offer an online commerce centre for sellers to run and market their products.

Although Etsy along with Amazon are the two biggest commercial sites on the internet, that doesn't mean there's not room for smaller commercial spaces and specialty centers.

StockX is an example of a less upscale special commercial center that allows people to market shoes.

stockx internet business commercial center for shoes

If you've got the idea of an online business center that you are certain would be successful There is no better time than now to make your website fully functioning.

Benefits of an e-commerce site

* Lower set-up and running costs than offline businesses The cost of the creation of an online website for your business is lower than separate associations. The entire arrangement system for your company is digital through the internet. This way, you will save money on pay, staff and other costs for business that are generally expenses like heating, rent, and force costs. The money you've saved could then be used to purchase the potential to be utilized to promote your business's website and product range even more. Websites for business can also aid you in growing your product offerings more quickly than you

would expect in a business environment that is not a part of it.

The Business Can be operated from anywhere Business locations that are online reduce any geographical limitations you'd normally encounter when operating offices-based businesses. You can be anywhere around the world and be able to operate your web-based business. The essential things you must have to be able to manage your business's online site from anywhere are shifting towards messages and messages, the Internet and mobile phones.

* Scale-limit: Business online sites are useful in that they allow you to determine the items that are selling effectively and ensuring that the stocks of these items are maintained. Also, how these attractive things can be expanded to increase the number of items to be sold through the website. This will enable you to expand your business to the degree of that you can increase your customer base, bargains and other benefits. Amazon's shopping site on the internet has been developed to be able to scale their product reach, as well as making sure they are constantly

checking what they are selling to customers. This has enabled them to effectively divide their range of products into distinct areas.

* No Restrictions on Opening Times When you have online business websites, you do not have to limit your customers who are regular, since they are able to access your website regardless of time. This implies that as a company you are expanding your options and benefits. What is the best way to ensure that your bargains will increase? This is possible through the use of various arrangements drives, such as amazing deals and electronic display drives. Some of the most important arrangements techniques you can make use of to build your online agreements include selling up and then systematically making pitches. Upselling is the practice of offering items that are directly related to products that the client has recently decided to buy. Items that are priced at a low cost meaning that the purchaser doesn't need to consider the 10,000-foot view and usually they complement the purchase they've already made, and make it a straightforward purchase choice. In this way you

allow the normal holders worth and make it more attractive. By consciously pitching, you can request that people spend more money through the purchase of more items. This is in the major aspect related to the that your client is buying. When it comes to online business websites, this could be described into a single phrase such as "You might also prefer", "Wear with this", "Ideal match with", "Why not go professional". These are all general methods to generate bargains for your company. It is also possible to make use of an array of amazing display promotions on your website to attract new customers to be a motivational source and outstanding, time-sensitive deals. They will encourage potential customers to act while browsing your site and, in turn, boost your conversion between visitor and bargain.

* More measurable than other Sales Methodologies: You could be wondering how I can believe it is effective How can I test the outcomes? Business websites can be tangible and easily measurable through the use of structures such as Google Analytics. You can view estimates

including the amount of inquiries addressed on your site page, average truck total the rate of surrendering a truck and the amount of total pay your site is able to achieve within the normal intervals. The costs for electronic business advertising are similarly less expensive than different kinds of evolving. You can employ the Search Engine Optimization method to improve the rank of your website's page on Search Engines. This could be a reliable monthly basis. Web optimization is an incomprehensible way to get more clients to visit your website.

* Less time-consuming: After your online business website is created, you need not require plenty of time and energy managing it. This is due to it being the entire process of customers mentioning their customers and creating portions of content will start with the online structure. This gives you the opportunity to pick new products that you must sell or unique offers to send out and also to observe the effectiveness of your plans. It is also possible to select any example depending on what items are selling the most effectively. The other thing to consider are the escalating bargain

pay that online business locations provide. The main quality that you can obtain through websites for business indicates that your business will attract new clients at any point during the day.

* Greater Margins and better Cashflow: In the case that your business becomes registered and operates within the business trade area An online business website allows you to market at higher margins. This makes the benefits you earn from your items overall higher. The grocery store and portion options on these websites also ensure that you get an entire portion of the customer right immediately. This improves your payment especially when clients consistently provide you with portions in only a few bits. There are a number of robust portion structures that you can use on your business's website, such as; Paypal, Google Checkout, Sage Payment Solutions, WordPay and that's only the beginning. It will guarantee that every portion trade is efficiently arranged so that your company can benefit from the portion profitably.

Advantages of an e-commerce site

* E-commerce delays goods except when you're making use of a site to book the delivery of pizza, a web-based conveyance for business sites takes longer to get your products in your hands. Even using express delivery services, the fastest the delivery date is typically "tomorrow" (aside by a few Amazon products). However, if you find that you require pen because you have to write something at moment, you cannot purchase it from a website commercial site. Similar to the candy you have to take in now, a novel that you must read in the evening, birthday presents that you're looking for tonight - you'll get the idea. A possible exception to this rule is due to the technologically advanced items, e.g., a digital book or music album. In this instance, buying products from a the internet-based business could be faster than buying items at a retail store.

* Internet business does not allow you to try the product before purchasing: You cannot touch the surface of the garment you're looking to buy. You cannot test what the footwear feels like on your foot. You aren't able to "test" the fragrance you'll need to buy. The thought is there. The majority of

customers have to see the product prior to making a purchase. The web-based company doesn't allow this. If you buy a music system and you don't have the ability to play it online to verify that it's right? If you're buying an home theater system it is best to take a seat in the "experience focal point" that a few retail outlets have are able to set up.

Anyone Can Create an online website for business We live in an age when face-to-face facades for customers online provide you with the capability to create an online business store in a short time. I've tried it and found it possible to establish an essential shop in under 10 minutes. On the off chance that anybody could set up a store and I want to know that the shop I'm purchasing from is a legitimate one? The lowered barriers down to a section could be a huge remembrance for the arduous online businessperson. But for the buyer in the end, quality assurance can be an issue. This could cause customers to restrict their purchases to highly regarded businesses.

* Security: When you make an online purchase it is essential to provide at all times your

Mastercard details and the street number. A lot of times websites that are based on the internet could collect other information regarding your online activities and habits. It can trigger Mastercard fraud or, more seriously recognize the difference between robbery and fraud.

Step-by step instructions for creating an online store

Choose the Product You Would Like to Sell: While browsing the internet, you most likely have seen the appearance of numerous eCommerce websites that sell a variety of items. There are certain websites dedicated to selling a particular line of products or services, such as clothes or products for itinerary, design items as well as other such items there are other websites selling various things such as computers, cell phones as well as books, home devices and home theaters, CDs, helpful cameras, sports items such as. This one is akin to a huge department store that sells everything under the same roof. In the beginning, it is crucial to choose the item or service you may be able to sell on your website. When deciding on the item to exchange, it is essential to assess the interest of the community. Buyers will always want to purchase items from a local retailer regardless of whether they're online or not. Local businesses will always ensure faster delivery times, more simple installment terms, and earlier changes in the event of the possibility of off-base or inadequate shipping.

Choose your business model If you are an eCommerce entrepreneur you are able to choose your strategy in accordance with your needs. Perhaps you will sell only through your website or you could sell your merchandise through commercial outlets like Amazon, Flipkart, eBay and more. Additionally, you can sell your products across both platforms simultaneously.

* Choose a Business Name name and domain: Once you've decided on the scope of your business and your plan of action the next step is choosing the name of your business and register the domain. A business name should be appropriate to your offerings and easy to remember to your target market. Domains give you a persona and helps customers to find you online. If you're one of the companies with

limited financial resources it's appealing to purchase a generic domain. Giving an existing domain up name can make it easier to reach out to your prospective customers. As your business grows, it is beneficial to have a dedicated domain because it aids in improving the site and a simpler acknowledgement.

Select an eCommerce Site Builder Nowadays it's simple to create your online store using the help of eCommerce website developers like Shiprocket 360. This programmers online can create websites in just a few seconds, allowing you to begin selling products in just a second.

• Designing your eCommerce Store Your eCommerce site is your online store and must be designed to accommodate the needs of your customers. Your website should provide information about your sellable products and services. Images, descriptions, prices comments from customers and evaluations must all be included on your site page for directing prospective purchasers. Make sure that your site's homepage displays your products in a professional manner so that buyers aren't misled.

It is important to make your web pages and website appealing, as this is your image that is displayed to buyers online.

* Set up the Payment Gateway: For an online company, you must have a variety of installment options available to customers. The eStore developers such as Shiprocket 360 accompany devices that allow you to add these functions to your website in this manner. Customers should be able to make payments using Mastercard credit card, charge card online wallets and net banking COD, and more.

* Secure Your Website With the Installation of an SSL Certificates: On each site which transfer data on the internet, it is important to make sure that their connection is protected by an Secured Security Layer (SSL). The SSL declaration keeps your site safe and builds trust with your customers. Nowadays, Google suggests having an SSL declaration for every and every website.

* Choose your shipping provider: Once you start selling products on your eCommerce website it is essential to ship the items to your customers

using messenger services. Logistics aggregators for eCommerce such as Shiprocket are the ideal choice. They provide a range of delivery options to your merchandise at the lowest possible delivery cost, so you will get the greatest confidence in the offer you make.

Chapter 3: Website Hosting And Launching

What is what is a Domain Name?

The domain name refers to the name of your website that users enter into the browser URL bar in order to go to your website. In simple terms If your site was a home the domain name would be the address.

A more detailed clarification:

The Internet is a vast computer network that connects one another via a global cable. Each PC in this network is able to talk to other PCs. To distinguish them, each PC is assigned an address on the internet called IP addresses. It's a series of numbers that identify the PC that is from the rest of the web. An IP address that is normal resembles this:

66.249.66.1

Today, an IP address like this is extremely difficult to remember. If you had to use the same numbers to visit your favourite websites Domain names were invented to solve this problem.

In the event that you have to go to a website that isn't listed, you do not need to type in a lengthy sequence of numbers. You can instead go to it by typing a simple domain name into the address bar of your browser. For example, www.twitter.com

Do Domain Names Actually Work?

To understand the way domain names work, we will examine the way you can enter it into your browser.

How do domains work?

If you enter an address in your web application the program first makes the sales to an organization of people who form the Domain Name System (DNS). The workers then look to find the name employees associated to the space and forward the request to those name workers.

For instance, if your website is hosted by Bluehost the name of the worker details will look like this:

ns1.bluehost.com

ns2.bluehost.com

The PCs are which are overseen by your facilitation organization. The facilitating company will forward your message to the PC that is where your website is removed.

This computer is known as web worker. It is a powerful computer that has been developed (Apache, Nginx are two common web worker programs). Web worker currently receives the website's page as well as details related to it. Finally, it then transmits the data back to the software.

What can Domain Name Different from a Web Hosting or Website?

Website hosting. A website comprises documents such as HTML pages web designer programming, images, and finally. If you have a domain's domain as the internet address of your website web hosting is the place for your site.

This is the PC where the archives of your site are stored. These PCs are referred to as workers, and are used to assist in organisation. To build your site you will require names for space as well as hosting. Be aware that they're two distinct administrations and you are able to get these from two different organizations.

Now, you might be wondering, how will it go if you acquired these from two different associations?

It is essential to change the settings for your space name and then enter in the Name Server information given by your facilitation association. Name Server information identifies the location to send customer inquiries to your area's name. We recommend obtaining the name of your region and working with a comparable association. This permits you to efficiently manage them with a similar record.

Domain Names: Types Domain Names

Names of areas are open to an array of extensions. The most well-known is .com. There are many options such as .organization, .net,. television. data, .io, e.t.c.

It is important to look at the different types of space names that are offered.

* Domain Name TLDs with High Level

High level area , or TLDs are space extensions which are registered at the highest level within the framework of area names. There are a variety of TLDs available however the most well-known one is .com, .organization, and .net. Some TLDs are not as well-known and we do not recommend using them. For instance, .business, .club, .information, .office, and many more.

* Nation Code Top Level Domain ccTLD

High level area of the nation code or ccTLDs are country-specific space names that begin with the country code expansion, for example .uk to represent the United Kingdom, .de for Germany, .in for India. They are utilized by cities who need to target the specific countries of a.

* Supported Top Level Domain sTLD

Supported high-top space or sTLD is a type of TLDs which aid in addressing specific neighborhoods due to the expansion of the area. For instance, .edu for training related affiliations, .gov for the United States government, and .mil is for and the United States military, to not mention the military.

What is the best way to choose the Domain Name of Your Website?

Selecting a domain name It is currently over 350 million domain names enrolled and thousands more are added each day. This means that each of the top domain names are currently registered or are expected to soon be added. This forces new customers to come up with the perfect domain name for their website.

14 Tips to Choose the best domain name

When you are starting your blog, choosing a domain name can be a challenge due to the fact that you'd not want to make an error. To make it easier there is a basic 14-step system that you can follow to choose the perfect domain for your blog.

Stay to .com

Use the expressions you want to use in your search for domain names

Keep your domain name short

Reduce it to a simple language and then spell

Make sure it is unique and memorable.

Beware of hyphens when you are naming domains.

Do not send out more letters.

Let domain be expanded

Examining your domain name

Use domain generators for best name

Make sure you act quickly before anyone else does the opportunity

The best place to choose the domain name

Get a domain for free through web hosting

Most standard area enrollment focuses

1. Keep to .com

There's an abundance of domain name expansions in the market today, from initial .com, .net and .organization to niche extensions such as .pizza, .photography, and even .blog. For the most part, we would recommend choosing an .com domain. Although it can be tempting to create imaginative blog names based on new technologies, .com is at this moment the most established and reliable domain name extension. The more innovative space extensions such as .ninja or .photography could be misleading. Domains for websites are in a similar fashion the most crucial. Many customers, particularly those who aren't taught to enter ".com" in the top of each domain, without taking into consideration the bigger picture. If your site is something like Jane.Photography, and your customers incidentally type in jane.photography.com, they will wind up on a good page on photography.com site. It is safe to stay clear of that danger by utilizing .com. Furthermore, all wireless control centers typically include the .com button.

2. Make use of keywords in your Domain Name Search

The catchy phrases are a major part in the area. If you incorporate catchy words into the name of your location and on your website, you can improve the listings of your website. Alongside high-quality content and an amazing user experience, the use of catchy words within your region can aid in ranking higher on Google. It's not easy to secure a good space that is devoted to your desired keywords and they're not being properly utilized. It is important to think outside the box and incorporate your catchy words with other phrases to stick out.

3. Make sure your domain name is short

While catchy words are essential however, you shouldn't go wild with the length of your area. It's better to have your domain name simple and first. We recommend keeping your domain name under 15 characters. The longer areas will be more difficult for clients to keep in mind. Furthermore, they will also be more likely to make errors in syntactic spelling with domain names that are long, that could trigger incidents. This is why it's a smart idea to keep your domain's length to a minimum.

4. Make your Domain Name Simple to pronounce and spell

It is recommended to effectively use your domain name in writing or speaking in a similar manner. There is no way to tell whether you'll be drawn closer to sharing your domain name in relation to. If you're planning to make use of your domain to create a professional business email address, it must be simple and clear to anyone.

5. Make sure it is unique and brandable

Your domain name for your site needs be memorable. It's smart to look into other websites in your area and find out what domain names they're using. It would be a shame to accidentally copy a brand name or be reprimanded for copying a blogger. In the same way, you can select an area names that are more branded. Brandable names are distinctive important, clever, and smart. For example, "Amazon.com" is a considerably more brandable name than "BuyBooksOnline.com."

6. Beware of Hyphens in Domain Name

Don't make a name for an area that contains the use of hyphens. Hyphens could be an indication of spam domains which you don't want to be associated to. Hyphenated domains can also be prone to mistakes in linguistics. If you select a domain with hyphens as the space you require is already filled, then your clients will probably end in the competitor's website in the event that they fail to enter the hyperbole.

7. Avoid Double Letters

It's a smart idea to stay clear of spaces that have more letters since it can increase your chance of losing traffic due to mistakes in syntactic. For instance, a site such as Presssetup.com is more vulnerable to mistakes, which could cause busy gridlock. Eliminating duplicate letters can further make your domain easier to form and make it more brandable.

8. Allow Room for Expanding

It's easy to choose a domain name that's connected to your company's industry or strength as it thinks of your customers and what's the problem here. However, you do not wish to limit your drawn choices to a certain amount. For instance, a flower retailer might select the domain name orchidblog.com but they could have to begin writing a blog on different flowers that go with orchids. The area could hinder you from attracting visitors who are captivated by different flowers. Moving your website to a different domain is an incredible process and can lead the site to fall off search results when you fail to make it right. This is why it's essential to pick an appropriate domain name that is flexible all across.

9. An Investigation into Your Domain Name

Prior to registering the domain name, try to determine if there is an existing business that is using an identical name. You can conduct the search engine for brand names to see if there's at present an exact or comparable name that has been recently used.

Examine brand names in an effort to not fight domain names. You could also perform the Google search to check the domain's availability on popular social media platforms such as Twitter, Facebook, Instagram and more. If you were to use a similar or similar name might cause a lot of trouble but it can also cause real and genuine repercussions that could cost the amount of money you spend.

10. Make use of Domain Name Generators to come up with creative Ideas

At present, there are over 360 million registered domain names. Many people believe that all exceptional domain names are now already taken. Finding a single area name isn't the most pleasant thing to do. This is the place where domain name generators step in. They are free tools that look up catchy phrases that you have mentioned to discover a variety of domain name ideas.

Nameboy space generator device

We recommend using Nameboy that is the most dependable and known area name generator available on the internet.

11. Make a quick decision before someone else Does it

Everyday, thousands of domain names that are new are being registered across all regions of the globe. If you've found an area that appeals to you, you shouldn't sit in a long line. Domain names are just like land. A lot of people are searching for domain names with a good brand which they can purchase for better rates in the future. If you're not moving quickly you can ask anyone to offer your domain name.

What is an Internet What is a Domain Name Registrar?

Domain name registration centre is a business that allows the buying and enlisting of domain names. Domain name registrars in all countries are accredited with ICANN (Internet Corporation of Assigned Names and Numbers) which is a non-benefit organization responsible for managing domain names.

Domain name names help make the internet accessible to everyone. In the absence of domains, users will have to enter a lengthy sequence of numbers, known as IP addresses to access websites.

Domain names solve this issue by allowing sites to choose to use easy-to-remember words, such as Twitter.com and google.com.

What do Domain Registrars Actually Do?

Every domain name record is kept in a central database known as registry. To ensure that a domain name will remain in the memory, it needs to be added to that database, along with any other information regarding it. A center for domain name registration has been granted authorization by ICANN to modify the data of your domain name in the database to benefit you. A domain name registrar also offers simple-to-use tools to implement these improvements by using your web browser.

Step by step directions for Choosing The Best Domain Registrar

Domain registrars are not all granted the right to market all domain name extensions. For instance, certain domain registrars may only sell domain names that have a country-specific extension(like .io, .in, or .ly). Each domain enlistment centre could offer additional services along with the enrollment of domain names. Some enlistment centers might offer domains of a modest price as a limited time offer while other centers may offer free additional services to attract customers.

When choosing the most suitable domain name registrar, review the four criteria that go with it:

1. Evaluation and registration period

The most important thing to look over is the cost of registering a domain. For instance, certain domain registration centers might offer cheap prices upfront for first year, but their reestablishment fees could be distinctive and significantly more expensive. It is possible to register the domain name with one year. However, some businesses may require a more lengthy time to register, for instance, two years or more. Domain registration can be done for a name for up to 10 years in one go.

2. Domain Transfers

Domain names are able to be moved beginning with one domain registrar , and then on to the next. Normally, you don't need to move your domain immediately, however in the event you're unhappy with your local enrollment center, this option must be available. The most important thing to be aware of is that you aren't able to transfer your domain name within the first 60 days following the enrollment. The duration of this period is determined by ICANN. From then onwards you are able to change it to any centers you'd like to join.

Many domain registrars allow for the transfer of domain names without additional fee. Some may try to confuse the process by charging an added fee to get rid of domain lock. Make sure you study the procedure for moving domains prior to you buy a domain from an registry.

3. Domain Expiration Policies

Domain names are listed for a certain period of time. You are able to reestablish your domain's enlistment prior to its expiration date. If you fail to restore your domain then it will expire and anyone is able to join in it.

In the case of businesses, this means the possibility that someone else will take over your domain. To make sure this doesn't happen, you should create auto-restorations to your domain's name.

No matter if you utilized the programmatic recharging feature It is a good idea to review your domain enlistment centers ' lapse strategy. Some domain registration companies offer an elegant period of time even after the expiration. This period of grace allows you to reinstate your terminated domain name.

4. Extra Services

You might also want to look into the various services that are provided from your domain registration company.. While you may not require these services at this time, it's great to know that they offer these services. The additional services offered could include domain security and domain stopping, as well as extended insurance for lapses, which is just the beginning of an iceberg. Some domain enlistment centers even offer WordPress hosting services hosting services for email, web designers, and email advertising solution, but that's just the beginning of an iceberg.

The best Domain Registrars to Purchase the Domain Name

Selecting the right domain registrar will help you avoid potential future problems. It helps you secure your brand's name, and helps you move your website to a different host or a specialist co-op. With regard to the strategies we discussed earlier they are the best spaces enlistment services to buy the domain you want to register from.

1. Domain.com

In 2000, Domain.com was launched. Domain.com is perhaps the most popular domain name registrar around the globe. It allows you to register any high-level domain name extension (TLDs) as well as numerous country code high level regions (ccTLDs). Domain.com provides a quick domain search tool can be used for study of domain names. Their search tool can show you the most popular domains too.

You can access all the domain executive devices that you'd expect at a high-end registration center, including private enrollment whois security insurance free whois enrolling in mass, easy exchanges, DNS the board email account, email send as well as other administrations. You can also purchase web hosting through their company if you are interested in. If you have any questions or concerns, you can reach their customer service department via live chat or email.

2. Bluehost

Bluehost is among the largest hosting companies in the world and is an undisputed WordPress hosting partner. As part in their hosting service they also offer domain name registration. Additionally, they offer a number of features that owners of websites require such as the ability to create unlimited subdomains, security against malware for websites as well as professional messaging through G Suite (Google Workspace) and then a few.

3. Organization Solutions

Organization Solutions is one of the largest domain registration centers in the world with over 7 million domains registered through them. You can register a broad variety of domain extensions including the well-known .com, .net,

.organization, .business, .data, and, in general, any other special TLDs. Because Network Solutions is one of the most reputable domain registration centers, their offerings include Web hosting, web design web security tools including business email addresses Web-based promoting SEO benefits, even IT assistance.

In essence, as an independent company They can be your all-in-one source for your web presence.

Start by using their search engine for domain names to swiftly find available domains. They also show top domains in their results as well. Their base is accompanied by everything that you'd anticipate, like DNS the board and private enrollment, WHOIS protection and more.

4. HostGator

HostGator is another renowned company that provides site owners with a complete source for domain names as well as shared hosting. They provide a good selection of extensions, protection for domains and easy to use DNS tools for the executive. They offer a simple-to use tool for domain searches which assists you in tracking an appropriate domain for your company. Their domain is in the executive area. is a bit snobby and extensively recorded, which makes it easy to transfer domains if you require to.

Alongside hosting and domain names They also have launched an out of the box drag-and-drop web design tool named Gator. They do not offer domain names and hosting as part of their plans for web designers.

5. GoDaddy

GoDaddy is among the oldest and most well-known domain registration companies. They manage more than 77 million domains for more than 18 million customers. They provide a variety of domain name extensions to explore. Their prices are very competitive and you could enjoy a massive discount for the initial year of enrollment for your domain.

GoDaddy offers a simple to use interface for domains that allows you to transfer your domain's name, modify the name server, modify contact information, and alter various other settings for your domain. GoDaddy also allows you to set up a variety of additional services on the internet, such as web designer, hosting as well as email advertising. And this is just the beginning.

6. Namecheap

Namecheap is another of the top domain registrars available. They provide a powerful domain search tool that aids in locating the right domain name and also provides ideas for when your preferred domain isn't available for free. They also offer additional area services like domain protection as well as premium DNS. Their domain in the executive area is clean, however it's not as simple to grasp as GoDaddy's latest interface. The best part to mention about NameCheap is the fact that they provide free space security for every domain they own.

7. DreamHost

DreamHost is another well-known domain name registrar as well as a web hosting expert co-op. DreamHost provides 400+ TLDs, and includes all domain-related tools that you could expect from a huge area provider such as DreamHost.

8. BuyDomains

BuyDomains allows you to search for premium domain names that match with your search terms. Domain names that are premium names that have been enrolled however are open to transfer from an outsider. They are usually more crucial, limited and identifiable, and that's why they're more costly.If you are unable to track the right domain and you're in the budget then you can utilize BuyDomains to find a more reputable domain name.

The Top 10 Web Hosting Companies that are the best

* Bluehost - The Best Web Hosting for beginners

* DreamHost - The Most affordable Month-to Month Plan

* Hostinger - Best Cheap Hosting Plans

HostGator is the best option for those who need to be lean or minimally strained.

* A2 Hosting - Reliable and Fast Shared Hosting

* GreenGeeks Greenest Hosting for Eco-Friendly Business

* WP Engine – Best Managed WordPress Hosting

* InMotion is the best VPS Hosting

* SiteGround is the best to Make Your WordPress Site Fast and Secure

* Nexcess is a great choice for developing and scaling

Chapter 4: Wordpress

What is WordPress?

WordPress is a completely free open-source website creation platform. At a higher level, WordPress is a content management system (CMS) built in PHP which uses an MySQL data base. In non-greek terms, WordPress is the simplest and most significant contributor to a blog or web designer that is available at present. WordPress is an ideal website platform that can be used for a variety kinds of sites. From blogging for a blog to e-commerce, business and portfolio websites, WordPress is an adaptable CMS built with the idea of ease of use and flexibility, WordPress is a fantastic solution for small and big websites.

A WordPress website is a site which uses WordPress to manage its contents system(CMS). WordPress is the engine behind both the backend of your website (the user interface that a visitor is able to sign in to make changes or to add content) as well as the frontend (the visible part of your website that users see on the internet).

Here are a few examples of of sites you can create using WordPress:

* Blog A blog is a fantastic type of site that is dedicated to sharing thoughts photographs, images, surveys training exercises, etc. The majority of websites display the most authentically conveyed information first.

* Web-based business website A website for business online permits you to sell items or administrative services online and to collect installments using an installment platform online. You can download and implement the WordPress online business module to increase the functionality of WordPress and allow you to run an online store on your website.

* Business websites: Many organisations will gain from being online through their own web site. If your company requires a website that customers can visit to obtain details about your business and what you want to offer, WordPress is an astonishing alternative. Customers can get in touch with you, request an affirmation and plan a strategy and much more.

* Enrollment sites A participation site permits you to use the content on a paywall, or an account record. To make posts or pages users must sign in to pay for content. WordPress is able to manage enrollment locations with additional modules.

* Portfolio website showcase your impressive design, planning skills and much more by creating an online portfolio website that is built on WordPress.

* Gathering sites A site for conversation could be a good place for customers to make requests or provide directions. You may be surprised to learn that many chat rooms run on WordPress.

* Event site hosting an event? : WordPress simplifies it for you to publish the details of your event and to sell tickets.

E-learning websites students can access online courses, follow their own events, download materials and much more from an online learning website. With this amazing module, called the WordPress LMS module that allows you to offer online classes on an WordPress website.

* Wedding site: Tell the world about the nuances of your special day by creating a wedding website built on WordPress. With a wide range of WordPress wedding-related points it is possible to get the site up and running without difficulty.

What exactly is an WordPress website?

The possibilities are endless in regards to modifying an WordPress website. WordPress themes as well as plugins are able to provide new plans and additional functionality. Visit WordPress.org in the hope of finding WordPress themes that are free and also plugins.

Is WordPress the right choice for me?

If you're seeking out the reason WordPress is a widely utilized framework for managing content on a site Here are some of the advantages for WordPress as a stage for sites:

Simple: WordPress licenses you to share and host your site's content swiftly. In all likelihood no matter how new WordPress user, you can without doubt utilize WordPress.

* It is absolutely free: The original WordPress programming on WordPress.org is available for downloaded and used. However, you are required, however, to pay for web hosting and a domain name.

• Flexibility WordPress lets you create various types of websites including single web diary sites and online stores to newspapers and magazines.

Simple to use If you have Word getting ready software such as Microsoft Word, you can build and manage a website.

Open source programming WordPress can be described as open-source software that is licensed by the GNU General Public License (GPL) This means that it's not backed by a single connection or a particular substance. Many developers and users group together and contribute to the program to improve it. The spirit of open-source lies in regular updates, obligation and free access for all.

* There's no convincing reason to be a coder WordPress does away with the fundamental of knowing the basics of programming to create an

online site. Although WordPress makes use of a variety of programming languages There's no reason to master any one of them in order to use WordPress.

It is extensible with WordPress module: core WordPress programming language can be integrated to WordPress plugins. WordPress modules are pieces of code that you can add to your site to include additional features, (for instance, online business SEO, reinforcement, contact structures , and that's only the beginning). There's a vast array available for free WordPress modules accessible on the WordPress.org catalog of modules and an expanding premium (paid) module industry.

It is extremely flexible With WordPress subjects: WordPress subjects give the layout and design of your website. With just a click of an option, you are able to modify the look of your website by utilizing another WordPress subject. Additional created WordPress topics can be more similar to WordPress page developers, offering the user a greater control over your site's design.

* Site security Although there is no way to guarantee that a site will be 100 100% secured, WordPress security continues improving with the careful gathering of the focus's users and the originators. Important WordPress security concerns are usually due to botches by users instead of the actual issue.

A flourishing local region of creators and customers If you have your own WordPress website, you are able to as well participate in the bigger WordPress social group via your nearby WordPress Meetup, WordCamps and that's just the beginning. The WordPress social group remains very welcoming, consistent and creative.

Premium modules and subject market: While there are a lot of free topics and modules the majority of accredited WordPress owners of websites put their assets to premium (paid) modules or subjects. Why? The purchase of a premium topic or module can help fund the constant developments and the ongoing sponsorship of the subject or module that includes updates, security improvements and new highlights to name a few.

WordPress Features

As a stage for building websites or CMS, WordPress displays a important list of its highlights. Below are a few of the many advantages of WordPress.

* Website design enhancement The process of Search Engine Optimization (SEO) starts at a specific level, and WordPress provides an amazing code base to support SEO. Web streamlining permits your site's content to be found by an important internet search engines like Google and Bing.

"Speed: WordPress is a lean website framework that is always trying to remove the code "swell" which hinders the speed of stacking the site.

"Portable agreeable: The majority of WordPress subjects are today able to be adapted heartfelt and flexible out of the box.

The library of media reports: WordPress integrates an existing media library, allowing you to move and embed media data like images or accounts in your posts or pages. It is also possible to make fundamental modifications to your images within WordPress.

Simple to use: UI WordPress isn't hard to use and doesn't require any complicated settings. In the event you are able to use the WordPress processor you may make use of WordPress. WordPress also takes into account about the availability.

• Custom Menus WordPress makes it easier to create route menus using associations with your pages, or even custom associations.

* Inborn blog. Adding blogs to your site is as simple as the process of distributing a article.

* The new feature in WordPress 5.0 WordPress Block Editor WordPress Block Editor WordPress 5.0 introduced the brand-new Block Editor, in any instances referred to as"the Gutenberg WordPress Editor. The new editor's supervisor alters the method by which you edit WordPress Pages and Posts.

About WordPress

WordPress was created in 2003, in 2003 when Mike Little and Matt Mullenweg agreed to fork a obscure method of distributing content to a blog tool called B2/cafelog. Little and Mullenweg wanted to create an even better contributor than a blog stage considering the B2 base code, however with more enthralling highlights and a more predictable turn of developments.

It's the result: WordPress. Beginning as a tool for writing for blogs, WordPress quickly created to become a vast substance cadre of executives (CMS) designed to handle a variety of sites.

WordPress.com versus WordPress.org

If you're just beginning using WordPress there are a lot of aspects to be aware of. The first is to be aware of the difference between WordPress.com as opposed to WordPress.org.

The difference between WordPress.com as opposed to WordPress.org is to some degree frustrating if you're new to WordPress.

WordPress.com is the facilitated version of WordPress that lets you create an

WordPress.com record to build your own blog or website. Obviously, your website's URL or area will join "WordPress," like myblog.wordpress.com. Paid updates will combine a customized area, Google Analytics blend, plus and the possibility of adding custom modules or topics, to at a minimum.

WordPress.com is owned by Automattic An association that was established by the principal WordPress producers, Matt Mullenweg.

WordPress.org is the place to download the WordPress software to install to your personal user or web facilitating account. The WordPress software is open-source and therefore is available to download and use. To be able to use the WordPress.org version of WordPress you'll need to have a domain name and web hosting from a legitimate organization like Liquidweb.

How do I get started with WordPress?

At present, you're wondering, "how might I start WordPress?" Again, WordPress is free. It's true, in truth, it's free. It's easy to start with the creation of a WordPress website that is at two or three levels.

There are some basic elements regardless of WordPress:

High-quality web hosting that facilitates

A space name

The WordPress program is a feature that you can embed to your website (most web hosts can handle the process on your behalf.) If you'd prefer to using the facilitated form of WordPress accessible at WordPress.com it is essential to create an WordPress.com list to begin.

What's a WordPress plugin?

An WordPress plugin acts as a collection of additional code that you can integrate into your site to incorporate new features, utility or integrate.

Modules can be installed through the Plugins menu on Your WordPress dashboard.

What are WordPress plugins? WordPress modules are pieces of code that are able to be changed to increase the capabilities of your WordPress website.

Introduce WordPress plugins. Installation of WordPress module on the website is an essential step.

Essential WordPress plugins for all WordPress Sites. All WordPress websites will benefit from these essential WordPress plugins.

* WordPress reinforcement module WordPress does not have a fundamental reinforcement system, therefore having an WordPress reinforcement plan in place can save you a huge amount of mental discomfort should you lose any information on your website. A reinforcement strategy is also essential to prevent the risk of a hack or security breach. BackupBuddy is the main WordPress reinforcement tool to help the site, make it more secure, and even move your website to a different hosting or location.

* WordPress security module WordPress security program, like iThemes Security endeavors to fix normal security flaws and protect your website against threats.

* WordPress SEO module WordPress SEO module similar to Yoast SEO will help you provide additional SEO (Search Engine Optimization) highlights and usefulness.

* WordPress structure module. Add the solid structure of your website like contact structures outline, move records, celebrate blessings and more . You can also use the structure designer module, such as Ninja Forms.

* WordPress business module that is web-based If you are looking to market administrations or products on your site by way of an online store you should consider a WordPress web-based business plugin. for example WooCommerce is a simple out necessity.

What is an WordPress Theme?

A WordPress subject defines the "structure" for your website. The majority of WordPress subjects provide:

* The overall layout (the appearance, feel and design) of your website

* Style styles that are printed across the entire site

* Concealing arrangement

The styles for blogs are set by posts and archives of blogs

* Pages plans (or formats

* Gadget regions

* Other intricate details

WordPress theme

Certain themes work as WordPress page developers, allowing you to design your own layouts for your pages without programming. Themes are added by using The Appearance >> Themes menu on Your WordPress dashboard.

By making use of the fundamental request using the fundamental request work, you can locate the free topic on WordPress.org. Topics can also be packaged into packs of records that are uploaded through the Themes > Appearance menu within the WordPress dashboard.

What is what is a WordPress Theme? A WordPress theme provides the completeness of the front-end design of your WordPress website. The majority of WordPress themes offer the general layout or style of your website, including styles for text, colors locations, contraption and page association (or settings) types for blog spaces and blog chronicles , as well as other explicit details.

Guidelines to Installing the WordPress Theme notwithstanding the default feature that comes with your WordPress base, you may additionally acquaint yourself with your own WordPress theme with changing the style and appearance of your website.

* WordPress Login Once WordPress is present on your web worker you will be able to access you WordPress login page by using two URLs that are outstanding.

Explore your WordPress Dashboard: The WordPress Dashboard permits you to handle all of the in-depth aspects of managing your website. When you figure out the way to navigate around this dashboard, you'll see the dashboard's simplicity to navigate and use.

* By using the WordPress Bar for Admin Bar or the WordPress admin Bar also known as the toolbar. The WordPress Bar for Admin Bar is a different zone that allows users access to controls in the background while you're at the top of the WordPress blog or website.

* Trying to figure out WordPress Settings WordPress has a huge array of settings to test the limits of your website.

* WordPress Pages and Posts When it comes time to create posts for your WordPress website, you have the option of creating a post or a page. Both have their own advantages and could be extremely interesting elements to your website.

* Adding Links to WordPress The WordPress page chief and post is enhanced to include hyperlinks to different pages within your blog post.

Add images to WordPress Utilizing a visual element such as a photo or picture is a fantastic way to clean up your blog page or post's content. Discover why it's normal to include pictures in WordPress.

* By using The WordPress Media Library The WordPress Media Library includes all of the files you've uploaded to your WordPress website The most recent trades are made first.

* Book WordPress posts Scheduling WordPress post scheduling is a straightforward method to ensure that your content is dispersed.

* WordPress Categories and Tags WordPress impressions and portrayals can be used to the reformist progression of the content of your WordPress posts.

* How to create an WordPress Page. Creating an WordPress page is at the most basic level comparable to creating a blog post. It is easy to understand the fact that pages are typically static content, whereas posts require a lot of time.

* Applying the WordPress Page Template A few WordPress subjects create page layouts that alter the manner in which your pages are positioned

towards the frontend (the part that is visible on your website). With the help of page arranges your WordPress subject will give you some freedom in how your pages appear as well as the places where specific page elements can be found.

* Administration of comments in WordPress Comments will add a lively conversation section on your website, allowing visitors to comment on your pages or posts.

* Adding Users to WordPress Clients in WordPress allows you the ability to add clients in various locations and benefits to your website. Once the account is created the client will require logging into your website using an account name and password.

How do I install WordPress

WordPress is widely regarded as the most popular webmaster in the world. It has control over 39% of the sites online. The guidelines are legitimizing that's because WordPress isn't difficult to establish and makes it simple for anyone to create websites. The top WordPress web-based facilitating organizations permit you to launch WordPress within a couple of clicks. In general the process of introducing WordPress is a simple collaboration that takes just five minutes to complete.

Step-by-step instructions to install WordPress easily WordPress

Things You Should Know Before Installing WordPress

Before you can introduce WordPress initially, you'll need an area name as well as an appropriate web-based facilitating company who is familiar with WordPress.

As this is a lengthy and thorough tutorial you can follow the links below to find the section you need to be in.

How do I Setup WordPress on Bluehost

How do you install WordPress on HostGator

How do I Install WordPress on SiteGround?

How do I Setup WordPress onto WP Engine

How do you install WordPress using cPanel

How do I install WordPress using Softaculous

How do I install WordPress using QuickInstall

How do I install WordPress using Fantastico

How do I install WordPress using FTP

How do you install WordPress on your Computer

How do you install WordPress in your language

How to install the WordPress Multisite Network

Things to do after installing WordPress

How do I install WordPress on Bluehost

Step-by-step instructions on how to Install WordPress on Bluehost.

Bluehost is a widely recommended WordPress hosting provider and one of the largest facilitation companies in the world. They understand WordPress all the way from beginning to end and are the most and friendly WordPress installation measure. Bluehost therefore, announces WordPress in your region name once you sign up.

After you log in onto the Bluehost account, you'll find your WordPress website under the 'My Sites Tab.

Bluehost Login to access your WordPress website

It is as easy as tapping on the "Sign into WordPress the catch and it will lead you straight into the WordPress administrator section.

In addition to their 'Essential' package, Bluehost likewise permits you to launch WordPress in a variety of locations through their various hosting plans.

Simply click on the "Make Site click on the button under the "My Sites Tab' to start.

Installing a the new WordPress site on Bluehost.

It will then start the Bluehost guide WordPress setup wizard. In the beginning it will ask that you provide a website title , or alternatively, an ad.

Add a title for your site to your brand new WordPress website.

Click on the "Following" catch to move on.

Then, you'll be asked to select the name of your area and the best way to designate your website. If you've purchased an area name then you can select it from the drop-down menu. You can usually purchase and add names for your area by going to the "Areas" page on the helpful dashboard.

Name of the area and basic modules.

Once you've selected the name of your space and a space name, you may keep the index path clear and let Bluehost select the name for you. The installer will also display some basic modules that you could introduce.

Now, you'll be able to click the 'Following' icon to continue.

The installer will create your WordPress website, which could take up to a few minutes. After that you will receive an elation message with your WordPress website's subtleties.

You'll also receive these alerts via emails. Then, you'll be able to click your login on WordPress catch to go to your new website's administrator section.

Congratulations, you've added WordPress to your Bluehost Facilitating account. It's not that bad, right.

* Instructions on how to install WordPress on HostGator

HostGator is yet another well-known WordPress hosting provider among the newbies. They also make it easy to get started with WordPress in just a few clicks.

For the first step first, you must log in to your HostGator recording's dashboard. From there, you'll need to click on the "QuickInstall symbol in the "Product" area.

We are introducing WordPress for HostGator. HostGator.

In the next screen, you must click on WordPress to launch the installer wizard.

Run the WordPress installation on HostGator.

In the next moment, you will be invited to choose the region name under which you must introduce WordPress and to enter the catalog method.

Choose your region's name.

Click on the catch to move on.

The installer currently asks that you fill in WordPress site details. It is recommended to enter an administrator username first and last name, and administrator's email address. Be sure to contact the email address because this is that you will receive your WordPress secret reset key email.

HostGator WordPress introduce settings.

After you have entered all the details, click the 'Introduce' link to continue.

The installer is running in the background to install WordPress to you. After the installation is completed, you'll get a success message with your administrator's client's name and secret code.

HostGator WordPress establishment is complete.

You will now be able tap the "Login" button to access the WordPress administrator area.

Congratulations, you've successfully created WordPress to the account of your HostGator account.

* Instructions on how to install WordPress on SiteGround

SiteGround is a popular option for WordPress novices. They are well-known for their outstanding support and their significantly enhanced WordPress using plans.

SiteGround provides fast and reliable free WordPress installers that cover all of their plans of action. It allows you to display WordPress clearly while working using the dashboard. We will demonstrate to you various ways to present WordPress through SiteGround. You can choose the one that you like best.

1. The presentation of WordPress at SiteGround as a new user

If you've just joined forces with SiteGround and SiteGround, you will receive an hello message upon the first time you log in. It will ask if you'll need to create your website right now.

New customer for SiteGround WordPress base wizard.

It is necessary to select "Start a new site" then click WordPress.

The wizard for installing WordPress will in the moment require WordPress basics. You must provide your email address as well as an administrator password, along with a private code for your brand-new WordPress website.

Enter WordPress login nuances to your basis.

Click on the "Insist" Catch to proceed.

In the next screen there are details of your guarantee. You can also pick other changes to your site, however we'll leave them out for now and you can include these later, if they are essential.

Complete WordPress foundations on a the new SiteGround account.

Tap the"all-out action" button. The program will through WordPress for you, running in the background. you will get a triumph message after it has completed.

Viably laid out WordPress on a new SiteGround account.

There's now the option of tapping the 'proceed to district of the customer. From there, you can track the new website under the "My Accounts tab.

Go to the WordPress director's board.

Tap on "Visit executive board' and enter WordPress manager location.

Congratulations! You've done a great job presenting WordPress on your brand new SiteGround account.

2. The presentation of WordPress for the first time on SiteGround as an existing customer

SiteGround allows you to be able to launch WordPress through your account in any point.

Simply sign in to your account and then go to SiteGround's cPanel dashboard.

Go to the cPanel dashboard on SiteGround.

It will also stack the dashboard of cPanel, which generally is an interface that is electronic to control the account.

From here, you must look down to the "Auto Installers Part and snap onto WordPress

Dispatch WordPress installer in SiteGround

The auto-installer will then start the script that has WordPress already selected. It is necessary to tap the catch that is currently on your screen and select a URL that is http or https as well as a space name.

At present, if you've activated SSL Certificate on the space name, you can select https as your domain name and choose http. It is possible to change later WordPress to HTTPS/SSL.

SiteGround WordPress Installer

In that section, you'll must enter your website's name Director username, Secret Word along with your email address.

In the same way, you will be faced with a variety of choices to select a languages, current modules as well as an indication of what's to come. You are able to alter these options , or just leave them as they are.

Finally, you'll be able to see you will see the WordPress Starter elective. It is important to be sure to check it as it will guide you through the present steps in setting up your website.

Optional settings.

In the moment Click on the "Acquaint" button and continue.

The installation will currently be running in the background and create an WordPress current. After the installation is completed, you'll get a win message that includes an official connection to your WordPress site's head area.

WordPress foundation is wrapped up

By pressing the name of your district manager button will bring you to your website and then run the set up wizard. One small step at a time wizard can assist you get started using WordPress. Press the Start Now' link to continue.

SiteGround WordPress start-up

If you do the starter wizard will ask you to select the best design for your WordPress website. It will provide you with carefully selected design templates that can be used by different classes.

SiteGround WordPress Starter Plan - Decision.

We suggest picking an arrangement that looks like the subject is your first priority. Check each subject by adjusting the options so that you are able to alter the look you see to suit your personal preference.

At that point you'll be closer to deciding on the functions that you should add to your website. This will typically be the 'Contact Form' option in light of the fact that every site requires the structure of a contact form.

Choose a your value.

In addition, it is possible to could select Shop (to create the online retailer) as well as timetable or JetPack.

Make sure to snap the capture to go on.

As time passes, you'll be more likely to make display options that will propel your site. It will provide you with MonsterInsights on Google Analytics, Yoast SEO and OptinMonster to determine lead-age.

We suggest you pick each of them three since they will assist you in growing your website.

From there you click the catch and the wizard will set up the foundation for you. Then, you'll get a win message that includes an entry into your WordPress dashboard.

Completed setting up your site

You can now access you are currently viewing the WordPress overseer dashboard, which includes customized substitute methods to create changes to your site's content, modify the plan and get started on your website.

SiteGround custom WordPress chairman dashboard

It's more than. You've successfully displayed WordPress in your SiteGround functioning with your the account.

Step-by-step instructions on how for how to Install WordPress for the first time on WP Engine

WP Engine is the best managed WordPress Facilitating provider. Oversaw facilitating accounts are basically an attendant service for your WordPress website.

They handle your WordPress website updates, setting up and performance improvement, while you concentrate on building your business. As an overseeing WordPress facilitator, WP Engine consequently introduces WordPress when you sign up. In accordance with your facilitating plan also, you can create additional sites whenever you'll require they.

In essence, sign in to the WP Engine dashboard and visit the "Destinations" section. There is a listing of all of your WordPress destinations. Click on the "Make Site" button to create a new WordPress introduction.

WP Engine make new site.

In the next screen, you'll be asked to provide the creation of your climate. Choose a name that will help in identifying this location and then click the "Establish Environment Click Here.

Create a climate on your WordPress website.

WP Engine will presently introduce your WordPress climate. It'll require some investments to allow DNS modifications to be able to spread.

In the next step, you'll need to go to the WordPress administrator area by clicking on the link on the sidebar. You will also be able to see your login credentials in full agreement.

Log in for your WordPress climate using WPEngine.

If you want to add space on your website, you'll must click on the connect space. Because WP Engine isn't a space enrollment center, it is necessary to set your region's DNS configurations at WP Engine.

In order to do this, you'll need the IP address of your website and the CNAME. The information you need is on the outline page of your website.

Duplicate the DNS information.

We will now tell you the most efficient method to input this information into Domain.com. The basic settings are identical to all area recorders, it is just a matter of finding your DNS settings.

Log in to the dashboard of your Domain.com account dashboard and click onto DNS along with Nameserver configurations for the region name.

Nameservers for Area DNS and settings.

On the next screen,, you will need to modify the record A with an @ symbol as its name. Click on the Edit button to modify the settings.

Change the record settings.

From then on from that point on, you must add the IP address that was provided through WP

Engine as this current record's value and then click Update DNS.

Supplanting A record esteem.

You must verify whether you have an CNAME record that has www in its name. If it is it, you must modify the CNAME record. If you have any other questions is to click on the "Add DNS Record" button.

Addition of CNAME record.

Include the CNAME subdomain provided by WPEngine within the field Value. Then then click"Add DNS".

All you need to do is successfully linked your domain address to the WordPress website that is hosted by WP Engine.

* The most efficient method to Install WordPress via cPanel

Cpanel is an incredibly well-known program used by a variety of web-based facilitating companies. It provides site owners with an easy interface online to handle their accounts for facilitating.

It's a single-stop access to a variety of useful utilities like auto-installer software that can help users in the introduction of WordPress.

Organizations can choose the auto-installer they wish to use. Most of the time, Softaculous, QuickInstall, and Fantastico are the most well-known options.

We'll tell you the most effective method to launch WordPress using each of the auto-installers. Follow the instructions, in respect of the installation you can see in the cPanel dashboard.

Step-by-step directions to Install WordPress using Softaculous

Softaculous is a popular auto-installer script. It lets you easily install popular web applications such as WordPress in just a few clicks. Facilitating companies such as SiteGround as well as InMotion Hosting use Softaculous in their control panel.

Log in to your cPanel record and then search in the search bar for Softaculous as well as

WordPress installer symbols. You'll find them in the Auto Installers area.

Touching each of them will trigger Softaculous Auto-Installer to WordPress. First you will get an overview of WordPress. Click onto the Install tab to move on.

Click on the Introduce tab to continue introducing WordPress using Softaculous.

Softaculous will now ask you to select the location where you want to present WordPress. Choose http://or http://www. to use the convention.

If your site is protected by SSL or HTTPS security, then you may select https:// or https://www. to use the standard.

From then on it is your responsibility to select the name of the area where you'll need to introduce WordPress. A majority of users need to introduce WordPress within their local root index, for example.com. There, you'll need to make sure that the field 'In Directory' is in order.

Take a look below and you'll be able to be able to see the settings for your site.

In this section, first you must give the name and description of your WordPress website. Be careful not to overdo it. will be able to without much effort change them in your WordPress administrator area after establishing.

In the next step, you must select the username of your administrator, the secret password as well as an email address. Softaculous will complete both the password and username key field for you. Softaculous will make use of the non-word word reference word to create a username as well as a secure secret key.

They can be changed to whatever you require so that they're not difficult to remember for you. However, we strongly suggest that you use an effective secret phrase. Read our guide to the efficient method of managing passwords for WordPress beginners to find out how to manage solid passwords with no issues.

Make sure you type in the correct email address into your administrator's email address field. This is the location in which WordPress sends out notices and the secret phrase reset connect in the event that you have failed to keep track of your secret key.

The other options that appear on the screen are optional. Then, you'll be able to click the introduction catch to launch the installer.

The decision is yours. WordPress settings within Softaculous

Softaculous will execute the installer using the settings you provided. There will be an improvement bar and an establishment status. It can take a few minutes. Make sure to not close the browser until the progress bar is at 100%. If it does or something else, as this could impact the performance of your WordPress website's performance.

You will get a success message once the installation has been completed. It will also show you connections to your website and with your WordPress administrator area.

Instructions on how to install WordPress by using QuickInstall

QuickInstall is another popular auto-installer used by a variety of facilitation companies such as HostGator and many more. HostGator's cPanel dashboard in the screen shots in this article, however it would be any different on the possibility that you're using any other hosting service that supports QuickInstall.

First you will need to log in to the cPanel dashboard of your facilitating record. Navigate to the Software section and then you click the QuickInstall symbol.

You will be taken directly to the 1 Click Installers web page on QuickInstall. It provides establishments for the most popular web applications, including WordPress. Click on WordPress to launch your WordPress installer.

Choose WordPress to establish the site.

The installer will display an overview of the WordPress outline. You will then be asked to select the name of your space beginning with the drop menu.

Dispatch WordPress installer in QuickInstall

Now click the next button to continue. The installer is now asking you to enter WordPress details such as the username and email addresses and website title.

QuickInstall WordPress site settings

After entering all the information after that, click on"Install..

QuickInstall will now launch WordPress to you. From then on you will receive an excellent message that includes the details of your login, such as username and secret code.

WordPress was successfully launched using QuickInstall.

Now, you'll be able to click the "Login" button to access the WordPress administrator area.

All you need to do is have successfully introduced WordPress using QuickInstall.

The steps to build a website using WordPress

Stage 1. Stage 1.

One of the most well-known mistakes that newcomers make is selecting an unsuitable site stage. The good news is that you're here to avoid the same mistake.

For most users using a self-hosted WordPress.org website is the best option. It comes with a variety of add-ons and plans that let you create any kind of website that you'd like to. For more information on this subject If it's not too difficult check out our guide to the reasons you should use WordPress.

WordPress is completely free for anyone to download and create any type of website, without restrictions.

If WordPress is free Where is the cost being sourced?

WordPress is free because you'll need to create your own domain name and facilitate, which will cost money.

Space names are your website's address on the internet. It is the name that your customers type into their browsers to get to your website.

In the next step, you'll require the site to facilitate. All websites on the internet require facilitating. This is your site's home on the internet. A domain name is typically $14.99/year and the cost of facilitating starts at $7.99/month.

In the beginning first, you'll have to visit the Bluehost website in a different program window, and click on the green "Begin Now button.

Begin by signing up with Bluehost.

It will take you to a valuation page, which will let you select the best plan to evaluate your website. The most important and, as well as plans are among the most popular choices among our customers.

Choose your preferred facilitating plan.

You'll need to click on select to select the layout you prefer and then proceed to the next stage.

In the next screen, you'll be asked to select another name for the space.

Select the space's name.

In the ideal world, you should stick to the .com domain name. Be sure that it is identifiable as a business name, easy to write and spell as well as easy to remember.

Need help selecting the right appropriate name for your site's area? Take a look at these tools and tips for the best method to choose the most appropriate name for your area.

After selecting the name of your space Click on the next button to continue.

In the next step, you'll be asked to provide your personal information such as name, address email address and more.

On this screen, you'll be able to see additional products which you can purchase. We generally do not recommend purchasing these products. It is possible to add them in the event you decide that you require these items.

Uncheck any additional items that are discretionary.

After that, you'll include your installment details to complete the purchase.

When you've finished your purchase After you've finished your purchase, you'll receive an email with hints regarding the best method to log in to your web controlling panel (cPanel).

This is your dashboard which you can manage all the things includes getting support or establishing messages and so on. Most importantly this is the area where you'll present WordPress.

Stage 2. Introduce WordPress

There are a lot of icons to perform different things on your facilitation accounts Dashboard (cPanel). There is no need to use the majority of them, therefore you can safely ignore the rest.

Find the site section in cPanel and then click"WordPress" WordPress symbol.

Introduce WordPress

You'll now see Bluehost Marketplace Quick Install screen for WordPress. Click on the 'Begin' button to begin.

On the next screen, you'll be asked to select the name of the area where you will need to announce WordPress. Select the area you want to introduce WordPress from the dropdown and then click Next.

Select the name of the region

Now you'll need to enter your website's name along with administrator usernames and a secret code for your website. Do not worry about it as you can change these in the future within WordPress settings should you're required to.

It is also necessary to verify all checkboxes on the screen. Then click the "Introduce" button to move on.

WordPress introduces settings

Speedy Install will presently begin the process of introducing WordPress on your website. It will then provide you with layouts you can put to your website.

There's no need to make that mistake right now as we'll explain to you how to find and implement a the free WordPress layout to your website in the following guide.

After the installation is complete when the establishment is completed, you'll see a congratulations message at the top of the header.

WordPress introduces the most fruitful

You must now click on the 'Establishment Complete Connection', and it will bring you to the screen that displays you WordPress login URL as well as your secret code.

WordPress login URL and certifications

Congrats! Congratulations! You've created your first WordPress website.

It is now possible to navigate your WordPress account login screen. Your login URL will resemble this: http://www.yourdomain.com/wp-administrator

You are able to log into your WordPress website using your administrator's username as well as the secret code that you have entered prior to.

Stage 3. Choose Your Theme

The appearance and style of your WordPress site is limited by the design of a WordPress topic. WordPress subjects are carefully planned designs that you can incorporate on your site to alter the appearance of your site. Naturally every WordPress website has a primary theme. In the event that you go to your website it'll appear like this:

But don't worry because there's a vast amount of paid and free WordPress topics you can include on your website.

You can modify your subject via your WordPress admin dashboard. Click on AppearanceThemes and then click the 'Add New button.

On the next screen, you'll be able to browse through 4,492 free WordPress topics available through the official WordPress.org subject index. You can sort them according to the most popular, latest, and highlighted, as well as other elements channels (i.e design, industry, and so on.)

Need help choosing an appropriate subject? Take a look at our list of these fantastic topics for free WordPress topic for business.

It is also possible to study our article to the most effective method of selecting the best WordPress theme for your website.

If you are aware of that the subject is a subject that you want to discuss to the world, then you can find it by entering the name of the topic in the search box.

WordPress will display the topic in a list of items. Then, move your mouse to the topic , and then click"Install.

Introduce the WordPress topic. WordPress subject

Once you've presented your subject, you are able to change it by clicking on the Customize interface within the menu for Appearance.

This will trigger the topic customizer to where you'll need to modify your topic settings and live reviews of your website.

Modifying your WordPress subject

It is not necessary to set the topic's settings right away. You'll need to make it better when you've got some content on your website.

Stage 4. Include Content on Your Website

WordPress comes with two standard types of content, namely pages and posts. Posts are essential to a blog and appear according to a sequence of request (fresher things are first shown).

Pages are designed as static "one-off" kind of content such as your about page, your contact form, security plan etc. Naturally, WordPress shows your blog posts on the primary page of your website. It is possible to change this, and have WordPress display any page as the primary page of your website. You can create a separate site for your blog area or news area. It's true that you can create a website without a blog section in any way.

In that case what if we added something of substance to your website.

The first step is to add two websites to your WordPress website. Don't be stressed when you require more content for these pages at this point. It is possible to modify and refresh them as needed.

Navigate to Pages» Add New Page in WordPress administrator area. This will take you onto the page management page, which appears similar to this, based on the subject you are discussing:

A second page can be added

The first step is to assign a the page a name and then we can call the page "Home".

Once you have that, you can then insert content into the word processor underneath. You can include images, joins, text and recordings, as well as audio, and so on.

After you have added the content on your site, you are able to hit the distribute catch to put it on your website.

It is possible to rehash the experience by adding additional pages to different areas of your website. For example, an about page, contact us, or even blog pages that display blog posts.

We should be adding two blog posts also.

Visit Posts > Create New from your WordPress administrator area, and you'll see a screen like the one you had seen before adding pages.

Add another blog entry

You can create the title of your post, and later insert content into the visual proofreader. You'll also see additional alternatives in the sidebar such as posts' classifications, post organization, and labels.

Tap onto the save catch and save your blog post in draft form or snap on the distribute catch display it on your website.

Stage 5. Revamping and tweaking your Website

If you've created certain content on your site You will want to modify and get things in a good design on your site.

What about starting with the first static page?

Set up the Static Front Page

You must go to the Settings >the Reading page within your WordPress administrator area. Under the heading 'First page showcases alternative, click on the static page first and then select the 'Pages' that you have created before for your blog and home pages.

Static's first page

Be sure to tap on the 'Save Changes' button on the bottom of the page, to save your modifications.

WordPress currently uses the Home page as your homepage's main page. The second page is 'Blog' to display your blog posts.

Change the Title of the Site and Tagline

When you create your site, you select the name of your website. WordPress also incorporates a slogan into the site's title, which reads "Just another WordPress website'.

You can alter the title and slogan of your website anytime by going to Settings >> General.

Title of the site and slogan

Your website's title is what you call your website as WPBeginner. The slogan typically is an a single line that represents the site's image. It is also possible to remove the slogan line should you want.

Be sure to tap on the save changes button to save your settings.

Configure Comments Settings

WordPress includes an underpinning commenting system that allows your customers to leave comments on your articles. This is a huge benefit for customer commitment, but it's targeted by spammers as well.

To control this, you'll have to allow remarks on your website.

Check the Settings > Discussions and then scroll down to the "Before a comment appears' segment. Look for the box next to the 'Remark needs to be supported physically.

Empower control of remark

Make sure to tap the save change catch to save your settings.

Create navigation menus

Route menus let your customers to browse through different pages or sections of your site. WordPress comes with an incredible menu structure, and your WordPress website makes use of this framework to display menus.

Menus for routing on a website

We could add an option menu for routes on your website?

To begin first, you must go to the Menus >> Appearance. Select a name to be used for your menu route and click the make menu button.

Making a new menu

WordPress will soon be a part of your menu of routes. However, it is empty at the moment.

You must then select the pages that you wish to display in your menu. Then, click the Add to Menu button.

Add pages to the WordPress menu

You'll see your selected pages filling in the empty space on your menu. You can drag them all over and re-evaluate their position within the menu.

Select the menu option

In the present, you have to select a presentation area. The areas you choose are defined by the WordPress topic. In general, WordPress topics have a basic menu which appears at the the top.

Finally, click the save menu button to save your menu.

You will now be able to go to your website to experience the menu in real time.

For further point by point guidelines, refer to our child's guide for the best method to include a route menu in WordPress.

Stage 6. Introduction to plugins

WordPress Plugins look like apps for your WordPress website. They allow you to include additional features to your WordPress website. Think of contact structure, photo exhibitions, and more. At present, there are over 49,000 modules that are free to use with WordPress. Additionally, there are paid modules that are sold by other webmasters and designers.

With so many modules to choose from, how do you decide the best modules to include? We've got you covered too, read our guide on how to select the most suitable WordPress module.

This is a list of the most important modules you should include to your site as soon as possible. All of them are absolutely free.

Highlights

WPForms Lite lets you include a contact form structure on your WordPress website.

Envira Gallery Lite is a great way to add stunning picture exhibits to your WordPress website

MonsterInsights Connect your website to Google Analytics and perceive how visitors find and use your website, so that you can ensure they keep coming back.

SeedProd Create special designs and templates using drag and drop landing page manufacturer SeedProd.

Site Optimization

All-round SEO - Enhance your WordPress SEO to get more visitors from Google

WP Super Cache improves your website's speeds by serving reserved page

PushEngage helps increase site traffic by allowing to connect with visitors who leave your site. Pop-up messages are the top five spots for traffic on WPBeginner.

Security

Updraft Plus - Create programed reinforced bookings for your website

Sucuri - Review of security on websites and malware scanner

Chapter 5: Elementor

Elementor is a Web Designer plugin that works with WordPress that allows you to create pages visually and in a live manner. Elementor is an unbeatable and completely free WordPress simplified administrator that lets you build stunning WordPress websites in the fastest and most efficient way possible.

What's so special about Elementor?

The main difference is that you are able to be visible at a high degree of planning you are planning in real time, and also at the front end of your website.

Elementor is the first and currently the most competitive front-end page maker to offer an array of plan options. It integrates a variety of significant tools as well as an incredible collection of organizational tools, a small toolkit for changing and a visual history of revisions with. These are just some of the benefits that are available to you with this free plug-in.

What is the process behind Elementor Page Builder work?

Elementor is a page maker plugin that replaces the basic WordPress supervisor by an actual proofreader on the frontend which allows you to create complicated configurations easily and also plan your site live without having to switch among the management mode and audit mode. The page producer allows you to display an exceptional level of quality without having to learn CSS or code and also without relying on planners for assistance. The UI is extremely pleasant and takes just takes a couple of minutes to become familiar with. We've accumulated Elementor with the most recent advancements and have continued to improve it continuously since we released on June 16 and the entire page creator is advancing and swiftly responding. This implies, for instance that when you work with gadgets, the work is accomplished in a flash and without a lot of leeway in any shape or shape or.

How do I Utilize Elementor?

* Install Elementor

To install Elementor Make sure that there is a WordPress installation ready. On your WordPress dashboard, click the 'plugins' tab, then 'Add New to your dashboard' and type in 'Elementor on the search bar. Then click the 'Install' link then click activate the button.

* Edit another page using Elementor

Navigate to 'Pages' > "Add New". Then you can click the 'Edit using Elementor click.

* Addition of the Elementor Template

Now you should be in Elementor. Elementor editor. Select 'Add Format' and choose from the large collection of templates, both paid and free. It is suggested to begin with a template so that you can become more familiar with the various elements of the site are designed.

* Make the template wide.

You can stretch any page Elementor fully-width by clicking Section > Layout and change the stretch section to Yes.

Learn the basic design of Elementor.

Every Elementor page is made up of sections, areas, and widgets. Segments divide the page into columns that are even. Segments divide the segments into sections that are vertical and widgets are inserted within the segment.

* Add an element to your widget

Let's take the chance of incorporating another widget to an existing page. Remove one widget in the format you've integrated using the click on gadget. Then following that, click on the X symbol. In the left panel, search for the button widget , and drag it to the empty area where you've just deleted the widget.

* Change background image

Select one section. This will display the section's setting on the left side of the board. Select the middle "Style" tab, then select the background image. Now, select a new image, and click 'Embed Media'.

* Change font

Click on the head widget in the webpage, and click it. This will display to the settings for headings on your left panel. Click on the center Style tab, then select the option 'Typography'.

Now, under "Family," you are able to explore the different fonts and choose a font from the family.

Inside Hello Theme

What can make Hello Theme so exceptional for web designers, besides the speed and lack of puffing clearly, is that you receive six major designs that are incorporated into:

The default template The default template is the main layout and has the sidebar as the right

Full Width page: Make use of this page to avoid having the sidebar appearing and tilt towards the main body to cover 100 percent of the width

Pages Left of the Sidebar: If you want to change the status of the sidebar

The Page Builder Blank is perfect for places of arrival because you have a brand new starting point, with no header or footer. Create the entire page using the page creator

Page Builder Boxed This is a rare beneficial configuration as it eliminates the page's title and all associated extra spaces

The Page Builder Full Width is like Page Builder Full Width, which is similar to Page Builder Boxed theme, however , the content spans the entire length of the screen.

wordpress-dashboard

Page Builder for Hello Theme

The cost-free Elementor page maker is the best choice for Hello Theme, and adds an extensive list of capabilities that takes into account the work of the webmaster. It lets you create your site much quicker than the other timeframes in memory that is late. The highlights include:

* Editable Adaptability to clearly make the page 100% flexible and adaptable

* Designs that are pre-arranged to allow you to quickly your action for a spectacular

* Page plan with one tick

* Effects such as Box Shadows and other activities give the pages truly magical

• Design Library to store your pages for future use and to transfer

Numerous helpful tools like Testimonials and Counter

* Live frontend design control that allows you to determine the layout of the page in the frontend

01. Frontend Live Page Designs

There have been various attempts over the years to create an WordPress page developer that chip away at the front end - giving you the ability to modify elements on your page without having to view the site live. Elementor is simple to implement it. There are no slacks or confusing gadgets and there's no compelling reason for switching into see mode. and no lengthy expectation to master and adjust. Every plan element is updated constantly and continuously.

02. Authority Over Layout

A remarkable plan begins by constructing the page. Making sure that the various page components and the gaps between gadgets as well as their dimensions, size and positioning, could be the decisive factor in an idea. Elementor offers you more control over these settings than anything else since the dawn of time an active page creator for WordPress. Since it's a live-developer it's much easier to select whether the unique configuration settings for your page are generally customized to your preferences.

The page area of Elementor is the core of the page. They let you reach the level of configuration that was previously reserved to date for expensive, specially-designed websites.

* Resize segments

The process of experimenting on the size of segments is never easier. Grab one of the corners and drag it around until you have the perfect section layout.

* Elementor segments hole

Make holes in the sections so that your plan to ease. By replacing the holes quickly it is possible to decide which has the best fitting.

* Content location

Place the segment at the top, the focus or the lower portion of a segment. You can also extend it to the whole segment. It is also possible to locate the content within the segment in the same method.

* Elementor strach sections

Create edge and cushioning on devices, segments, and areas by using the following options: px, EM or percent. Our dynamic size settings allow you to monitor the show on various screens, flexible or even something else.

03. Power Over Styling

* Page Builder for the WordPress board

The Elementor tool lets you modify the style of each device that you add to the page, similar to how you do for sections and lines. This control for styling incorporates modifications of textual styles, tones, the foundation and division. Do you want to alter the look of a fish? It's possible to do it with an easy drag on an oar.

* Typography

Explore more than 600 styles of text. With Elementor you have a range of control options for typography that are suitable for every device and area of the web page. Investigating with different letters dispersing, line height and textual style weight changes in text (capitalized or lowerspace) Italics, and that's only the beginning.

* colors

Elementor lets you maximize the range you have created and apply it on every page you create. This helps you keep your plan in place and to maintain a solid branding. You can also select any shade you'd like to think about using our color selection tool or by putting in the Hex code. With each tonal, you have the option to choose the level of obscurity or shades that are cloudy.

* The foundations and boundaries

Foundations are among the effective method of creating stunning and captivating page designs. With Elementor it is possible to set the foundations of your images or shades for each segment or section. Additionally, you can create video foundations, select between your own self assisted recordings, or even install YouTube to play on the back of the scene.

Draw boundaries and define line spans in order to properly outline your material.

* Dividing

There are two distinct degrees of dispersing opportunities for technology:

Separating the gadget from various gadgets within the section. Control the edges and cushioning of every gadget. Left, right, top and right are able to be set in a separate manner.

The division of components within the gadget. The counter device can, for example, allow users to adjust your distance to the counter and the content number.

* symbol

Textual style great symbols

Explore over 400 intriguing symbols and alter them to suit your personal design. Make use of Icons in order to create a site look more appealing and engaging.

04. Each of the Widgets You'll Will Need

With Elementor you can enjoy the complete array of devices, all absolutely free. There is no other page maker for WordPress has ever provided a variety of tools for free. These gadgets comprise standard devices such as heading, content or picture frames, as well as additional advanced gadgets such as video foundations, switches and accordiontechnology, Google Maps, and other.

05. Any Theme or Plugin Any Page, Any Theme

The similarities begin with a very designed code. We've created Elementor as refined and subtle as it can be It's fast and isn't a struggle with various subjects and modules.

Elementor can be a challenge on every subject, which means you can use the most popular topic planand modify your page's layout faster than you ever have with Elementor. The most significant benefit of using Elementor to create your web pages is that they remain in your mind regardless of whether you buy a different topic or in the event you decide to create your own customized topic.

Similarity of Elementor to modules such as Woocommerce, WPML and Yoast which means you're safe from conflicts, but you shortcodes can be moved from other modules that you're currently using.

Do not agree to only planning posts and pages. Elementor allows you to design any kind of post that you may be using like pages for presentations, landing pages, portfolios, post, or other items.

06. Designer Page Builder for WordPress

We're delivering Elementor as an open source project and GPL as well as a major element of why that we're doing this is to make use of the power of the WordPress developers local to the area for a way to enhance Elementor considerably. We require engineers from all over around the globe to contribute to Elementor and contribute to making it a complete tool for professionals working on websites. Here are some other features that make Elementor design friendly.

"Clean code" and amazing engineering of code

It is a component that is often neglected by most users but truthfully it is the most important element that makes up Elementor. The extremely well-crafted code design is the feature that distinguishes Elementor and is able to take into consideration various aspects like moment-instinct and the similarity to other modules and subject matter. As an open source product as well as GPL, Elementor allows WordPress developers to develop and enhance it.

* Search Engine Optimization

This is in direct line with the information we discussed earlier about clean code. Elementor relies on the best recommended coding standards, which makes your website SEO optimized from the beginning. The next page created using Elementor will also come with speedy burden times an essential element in SEO.

* Custom CSS

Even though the styling settings must suffice to create an perfect plan, you could at any time set your own CSS in each device.

Chapter 6: Traffic Generation Strategies

Making blogs more popular is much simpler than static websites.

This is in part because of the interaction and continual update of information and content that improves the search engine rankings as well as the multitude of blog communities you can join to expose your site to targeted, top-quality visitors from other bloggers as well as those who are interested in your industry.

Since your blog is optimized for search engines, you have to be sure to continue to incorporate your keywords within your posts in order to then maintain your position on search engines as well as be ranked within blogs, directories and different sources for traffic to the terms that are the most relevant to your field.

Whenever I create a new blog, the first thing I do is join http://www.MyBlogLog.com and create an online profile that showcases my blog and announces it to the blogging community.

With MyBlogLog it is easy to include a widget on your website , which will display your most recent visitors. as a result, when you visit other blogs, your blog will be included in the menus for navigation of blogs that are also using with the MyBlogLog tool.

Not only can MyBlogLog aid you in creating instant traffic for no cost and it's an enjoyable and engaging community to be part of.

You can browse blogs that are competing and conduct market research about what kinds of products are presented and which subjects are in high demand and come up with some ideas to help you design the most targeted blog that you can and be capable of retaining visitors and continuously encourage new visitors to browse your website.

Blog Commenting

An excellent way to bring specific visitors to your site, who are attracted to your blog's products and content is to comment on similar blogs within your field, and include the link to your blog within the comment or signature.

Try searching on Google for blogs that are related to your subject that relate to your blog. You can also look for blogs that are popular, have lots of visitors, lots of activity, and are regarded as as an authority in your field.

Be sure to participate in the threads and conversations and give useful suggestions. Do your best to assist people as best you can. The more you contribute positively to blogs and forums and forums, the more clicks you'll receive on the link to your website and the more traffic you'll receive.

Don't try to spam blogs by posting comments that have no value. For example, posting one-liners such as "great post". This won't work and nobody will click your link.

Make sure you are actively involved within the group and earn an image in helping others and you will notice a massive increase in traffic!

Submitting To Directories

There are many directories available that will let you submit your blog at no cost (there are also paid directories). This can help to increase traffic for your blog by having users browsing the directories and coming across blogs, it can aid in gaining backlinks for your blog.

Many blog directories have a high rank on their pages which helps you be found in search results.

Doing this manually is very time consuming and a bit tedious, so I recommend using a software tool such as Brad Cullen's free Directory Submitter http://directorysubmitter.imwishlist.com/ that will automatically do it for you.

Singing Your Blog

The pinging of your blog will inform search engines Search Engines of your blog's contents, since search engines are constantly scanning the web for any new information. When you ping your website, you can accelerate the process of having all the pages on your blog indexed.

There are a number of websites that post any new content on the internet. By pinging your blog you'll also be able to notify these websites of your latest material.

Here are a few free pinging services that can ping blogs:

http://www.pingomatic.com   http://www.just-ping.com http://www.pingthatblog.com

Social Bookmarking

If you social bookmark your blog, you will not just get more high PR backlinks, but you'll also receive more traffic due to people who find your blog on social bookmarking sites and then visiting your website.

You should save every post you create.

There are many websites for social bookmarking as well as web 2.0 websites available which you can upload blogs to. This can be extremely time-consuming, which is why I suggest you use some type of software that will automatically bookmark your posts automatically.

Here are some most popular ones, which are cost-free:

http://www.onlywire.com
http://www.socialposter.com

Remember, there's a plugin we mentioned earlier, which can automate submissions using Onlywire.com every time you post an article:

http://wordpress.org/extend/plugins/wp-onlywire-auto-poster/

Article Marketing

Article marketing is very well-known and has been an extremely effective method to not just earn backlinks but also to draw traffic from interested readers. The most important thing here is quality content that keeps the user wanting more.

It's relatively simple to create new content since you can simply use the content from blogs you've composed. Make sure to submit your article to the best directories of articles however, try not to overdo it in terms of content.

Make sure to revise your article in a way to spice the style and avoid repeat content.

Here's a selection of most popular directories that I suggest for article content:

http://www.ezinearticles.com
http://www.articlesbase.com
http://www.suite101.com

http://www.buzzle.com

http://www.helium.com

http://www.articlesnatch.com
http://www.goarticles.com

http://www.articlealley.com
http://www.articledashboard.com

How to Write an Article:

The headline is among the most important elements of your piece. You should try to design a compelling headline that entices readers. Here are some good ways to structure your headline:

Top 5 Ways to .... (using the numbers)

Would You Trade Your Boyfriend for $100,000? (using questions) Find the Secret Method to .... (using terms such as "discover," "secret," etc.)

Since submitting your article to multiple directories of articles at the same time can be extremely long and tiring Here's a free program to help you make this process easier for you:

http://articlesubmitter.imwishlist.com/

Video Marketing

Video marking is one of the most efficient and efficient methods to bring more traffic to your website. Video blogging is very popular and people prefer watching video over other media (e.g browsing articles).

If you've got a excellent video that is interesting and informative You could see many thousands of viewers! With this many people watching your videos, you'll be certain to see an enormous number of people who will click your blog's link. This is a huge amount of traffic!

Nowadays, people prefer not to read a long sales letters, they'd prefer to just watch a sales film. Similar is the case with the blog content you write. If you take the material you that you wrote in your blogs and convert every blog post into a short video, you'll be in a position to upload your videos onto video websites within a matter of minutes.

Additionally, you can embed them in your blog once the uploaded content is uploaded on YouTube (we discussed this previously in chapter 3 on Content).

Videos can also be good for backlinks as well due to the fact that video sites are extremely popular and have high PR.

There are 3 options for creating videos:

1.) Utilize a flip camera and take a picture of yourself or someone else.

2.) Record Powerpoint slides using Camtasia (or the free version called 'Camstudio')

3) Using Animoto http://www.animoto.com which can create videos for you in minutes for

free. All you need to do is upload your own images or type your own text into the video the video, choose the music and layout and Animoto will handle the rest (it's extremely simple).

Chapter 7: The Best Blog To Earn Money From

Effective Blog Writing

There are many methods for writing good efficient blogs. However, not all of them require the actual being in front of the computer and creating blog posts each day. There are plenty of blogging services that take over the task should you decide to use.

Personally, I would suggest making a template and then making it your own, but you can pick the approach is best for your. The main points in this case are conciseness and information type, as well as target audience and the quality of the content.

Brevity The secret ingredient

The ability to be concise, or short is something that a lot of commercial blog writers think of as a standard. In their search to find the ideal keyword ratio and adding the appropriate quantity of links to their products, they forget that they're writing mini-novels rather than regular blog posts. The typical blog post is between 150-500 words.

Anything less than 150 could be considered a microblog, while anything above 500 is forcing your readers.

This is, obviously entirely on the topic that the website. If you've got a science-related blog and you're discussing quantum string theory or physics, and you're able to write blog posts of 1,500 words.

Discussions of this kind require some explaining, and it's a challenge to create fluff for them. If your blog is focused on fashion it's unlikely you'll need to write very long articles.

Visual Cues

The majority of people do not have huge attention spans particularly when they're looking through websites. If your blog's content is visually big and contains a lot of text, a lot of people might subconsciously think it is too much and steer clear of it because they aren't interested in reading it. This is the reason it's important to keep your blog's posts as brief as possible.

If you are dealing with a topic that needs a long blog post, you can increase chances of having it read by visually dividing the blog post into sections.

It is possible to separate the blog post into two separate posts for part 1 and 2. If you put it in the perfect spot, you can let each blog post stand alone and readers will be enticed to read the remainder instead of being afraid to read everything at once.

Another option is to alter how long you blog post. Make use of paragraphs and make the hard return following each. If you are able to highlight key areas, use bullet points. Keep your paragraphs to no more than three lines, and stay clear of any type of text that resembles the size of a square block of text.

What's the Blog's Subject Matter?

Keep your blog focused on the topic is crucial, particularly when it comes to search-engine optimization. When your site is about editing videos, then it is important to expand on that subject, but don't go to far. The subjects that are related to it could be editing software for video techniques for editing, effects training classes, cinematography books and universities offering degrees in video.

Try to identify anywhere between three and five similar subjects within your blog's field and keep them in mind. If you regularly write about a particular subject and you have lots of links backs and appropriate keywords, you are better chance of being seen as an "expert" by search engines.

If your site for video editing is well-known, you may be able to get the top spots on search engines for phrases such as "video editing" or "special effects." It is also often referred to as being an "Authority" on a particular topic.

The most important benefit of using your niche, in addition to the search results, is that you attract advertisers within the area. If your site has top-of-the-line result in Google as well as Yahoo for results of video editing, that means you'll be appealing to any business that is looking to market video editing goods or solutions. Your worth will increase in your field and you may charge higher for advertisements.

There are also many more affiliate sales for products that relate to a field you're an authority in. People are more likely purchase a product when it's recommended by a well-known website considered to be an authority in the field.

It is not necessary the need to "nichefy" your blog's content when you have a popular blog. It is still necessary to keep your blog in an area that is somewhat focused, but you are able to

Make it more inclusive. You could, for instance, run a blog that is about visual art. In the blog, you can discuss editing videos and painting, special effects, drawing, and 3D art. The possibilities are endless however, you will still have the same theme that will be present in every post and updates will be based on.

It also reduces the likelihood to become an expert on a specific subject, but it does increase the amount of advertisers you can select from. There are times when having multiple advertisers is better than having many advertisers in one subject. For example when DVD sales are down when your site is focused on purchasing DVDs, then you'll have fewer advertisers.

If your blog is about purchasing all kinds of Media then you could fill in the advertising slack by partnering with various companies such as MP3 Distributors or Blu-Ray Player Manufacturers. What you don't get in niche sales you can make up for in stability. Multifaceted blogs are harder to set up and it is harder to achieve daily clicks, however the stability you gain from it will give you a better chance of growth and a longer-lasting existence.

Who's the Blog for?

This all impacts the intended audience. Who do you write for? Knowing who your readers is essential for getting any work done on your blog. A few important points to consider are The field they are interested in as well as their age, gender, and their education background.

Field of Interest

The first thing to take into consideration is what your readership is looking for. The blog you write about could be related to DVD's in general terms but who are you focusing on? Are you targeting those who are looking to purchase DVD's, or people who wish to create DVD's, or who would like to read about DVD reviews?

You can pick any of the three of them if you wish and your blog may be about DVDs in general, however you're likely to get more visits from returning visitors when you concentrate on a single subcategory of your primary topic.

It's an excellent idea to choose one or two subjects which are especially compatible. For instance your blog could concentrate on the review of computer components and also where you can purchase the parts at a reasonable price. This is an ideal combination as people purchasing computer components typically need to know about a critique prior to purchasing

(Likewise those who seek reviews are usually looking to buy). This way, you've identified the top two priorities and marketed to them. The last thing you want to do is posting off-topic content with items which could be categorized as larger category, but don't seem to fit within what you're writing about.

If you're targeting users who want to read reviews and buy PC parts, you should not post a random blog about a brand new PC game. It's a good fit in the general category of computers, but it's not related to the content of your blog.

This doesn't mean you shouldn't create off-topic posts, they just must be tied to the subject matter. As an example, you could want to create a blog article about a recall of the most recent release of a computer part or even a blog post about the exact set-up of the computer up by a famous or another person of interest uses. It's a good idea to feature interesting news items that are relevant to your blog, but aren't necessarily relevant to your blog since they add the blog with a variety of content.

Which Ages Are they?

It's not an ideal idea to exclude or exclude a certain audience , but this doesn't mean you cannot concentrate on a certain group of people and tailor your blog to appeal to the people they are. If your blog's subject is related to menopausal symptoms, then your ideal readers are likely to be women aged between the ages of 35 and 50 since they're the main kinds of women affected by menopausal symptoms.

In this regard that you shouldn't make use of the internet language that is popular among teenagers in the present. Your viewers aren't going to be impressed If you sound like their kids or grandchildren.

Instead , you should maintain your tone mature and write with an casual and friendly voice. It is possible to research other blogs catering to your age and learn the way that writers tailor on a specific segment of people.

Teens and young adults aged 16-24 are typically people who were born in a time when personal computers were ubiquitous and fairly inexpensive. They are familiar with internet slang and popular themes that are circulated on social media websites. Adults aged 25-39 tend to be older (if not by much) and may or might not be conversant with internet slang and other terms.

The people in this age group be more financially stable and a lot of people within this age range may have families. Adults between the ages of 41-60 often have families and won't be impressed by web websites that don't have a family-friendly feel.

Of course, these are broad guidelines the market for your blog's niche could be seniors who travel in baker gangs. Anything is possible. It is possible to conduct more thorough analysis of demographics and figure out how you can use these to your advantage for the most effective outcomes.

Does Gender Matter?

Marketing for a specific audience It is possible to do so. In general, the subtleties you adjust to gender differences are quite delicate. There are certain occasions where it really makes the difference. If your website is focused on finding the right prom dress, your market is clearly women (specifically teenagers) just.

This doesn't mean that ladies aren't the sole ones purchasing prom dresses, but that is the most of your affiliate sales and clicks are coming from and this is the audience you want to target through your blog. If your blog doesn't relate to a gender-specific product, then you'll need to easily decide for yourself whether you would like to target a particular gender.

Sometimes it is beneficial to target marketing to a specific gender. Games, for instance are usually targeted towards males between the 12-24 age category. This has been a industry norm for a long time, since studies show that the highest sales come from this age group.

Chapter 8: Research And Sponsorship

Blog sponsorships are becoming an online trend.

It's because increasing numbers of companies have realized the potential of a blog posts as part of their marketing campaigns. With blog sponsorship you will collaborate in close collaboration with the advertiser and highlight their product or service through your blog posts. Additionally your blog will feature the brand name of the advertiser and the logo of their company.

You could conclude a sponsorship agreement by segregating a section of your blog which is exclusively to advertise your product. This type of advertising on blogs is extremely effective in the event that your blog is extremely popular and has plenty of people who visit your blog frequently.

Another method to identify blogs with advertising opportunities is making use of keywords research. Keyword research isn't just used for affiliate marketing, but it is useful to find bloggers to advertise on.

Here's how:

You can begin by performing an internet search using the keyword you are currently using within your website.

* Check to see if there's any advertisements currently being posted using this keyword. If so Find out which businesses based on their web site's URL.

Contact them and ask whether they're looking to sponsor your blog.

Exchange Links

Other blogs that have exchanged links before with you could be a potential advertiser. If they visit your blog and decide to exchange link with it, the chances are they will come across your blog as filled with potential, and they would like to exchange links with you. Thus, you could contact them by email to inquire whether they're interested in putting ads on your blog.

Find Your Price

Before you actually engage in any advertisers, you might want to think about what price range. Unfortunately, there aren't standards for pricing on the Internet. You'll need to look around, conduct some investigation and test out your own website to determine the best rates to maximize your profits.

What you need to keep in mind that your overall popularity will determine what the blog you run can be "worth" for advertisers. If you're receiving thousands of visitors per day, and possibly hundreds of clicks per day, you're valued at a significant amount. If your website is only getting hundreds of visitors per day, you'll need to reduce your costs to keep up with.

An advertiser or sponsor is likely to want results from the money that he will spend on your site. this is reflected in the visibility (impressions) as well as leads (clicks and possibly sales). So, make sure that your advertising contracts result in a positive outcome.

There are many inexpensive advertising options available (e.g. Google AdWords), and you'll have to be highly competitive. If you've reserved a great space for your sponsors (sidebar or the header) you may be able to start charging 50 cents per click (More about this in the following section). If your blog generates 100,000 monthly page views , a banner ad in your sidebar will cost you around $50. Begin with a low price and work your way up.

Chapter 9: Blog Monetization Strategies

Now you've got your website that is fully optimized, tweaked, and stuffed with useful content and you've started to drive traffic to your site by through free resources like blogs, communities as well as social media, it's the time to turn your website into money making machine.

This is where things get interesting!

If you are looking to earn money through blogs online There are a variety of options that are available. As with normal websites, you can incorporate Google Adsense or other advertising platforms such as AdBrite or use CPA offers from other services such as CPALead.com.

But it doesn't stop there.

As blogger, you are able to earn money by advertising items that you are affiliated with on your site and by building your list of people you can market your own services and products to. You could earn money through joining blog project databases which pay you to write about new products or providing feedback on companies' products, or providing reviews on

172

behalf of other bloggers keen to gain more traffic through your.

Of course, the amount of income you make will depend on the amount of visitors you can drive to your site.

The higher the traffic is generated, the more profitable your blog will be for potential sponsors who pay for it And, naturally when you have consistent traffic, you could earn commissions on affiliate products purchased by your referral.

As blogger for more than five years, I always advise new bloggers to focus on increasing traffic before looking to make money from their blog.

You must establish an image within your industry create as many backlinks as feasible, and get your site's visibility to all potential clients as feasible before you begin to focus on earning money from your blog. It is essential to have a dedicated audience, a faithful following and returning customers who find your site useful, informative, and worth visiting often.

After you have established your position within the blogging community and have established yourself as a blogger, you can move on by incorporating money-making strategies in every aspect of your blog, however first, you must start by laying the foundations and work on generating constant traffic to your site.

In the end, at the beginning of your site, there are a handful of things you must consider that could be profitable in the near future. One of these is making the list.

If you already have the RSS subscribe option available on your site but you should move it one step further by creating an autoresponder opt-in on your website. This form will collect the information of your visitors and allows you keep in contact with your customers.

In this way it is possible to build a rapport with your market and after you've established this relationship, you are able to start earning money through direct sales such as affiliate products, referrals and affiliate links even before your website is producing a significant amount of traffic.

In order to do this, you'll require two items:

1) Code Banter's autoresponder plugin available free at http://www.CodeBanter.com

2) An Autoresponder Account, available at

http://www.GetResponse.com   or http://www.Aweber.com

With these two tools that you have, you'll be able to begin building your list of subscribers from the day your site is created. All you have to do is think about the "subscription lure" (also known as the "opt to reward") you plan to employ to get your readers to sign up for signing up to your newsletter.

The easiest way to do this is by purchasing rights to a high quality report from places like http://www.ContentGrab.com or in outsourcing the development of a free report or eBook from an experienced freelancer on websites such as http://www.Elance.com

If you're competent at writing and are able to write, you can save yourself the time as well as money writing an essay that is tailored to the theme of your blog. It is essential to ensure that the information you offer is relevant to the subject.

After you have your report completed, you are able to access your autoresponder account to create your welcome email. It is an introductory email that will be that is automatically sent to every subscriber when they confirm an application to be added on your database.

The email will be a thank-you note for their subscription and include a download link to the report.

Similar to making money from your site, you have to start by building an association with your audience to ensure that they trust your advice and view your site as a trustworthy source of information, advice, and details on the subjects that are of interest to them.

Spend some time interacting with your readers, providing them information, materials, freebies about tips and tools that can help them.

If you follow this strategy then it won't take long before you've got an ardent following of customers who are eager to open your emails, take note of your messages and seriously research the products you offer.

Affiliate Links

The most well-known affiliate programs that are available for blogs are Clickbank, Commission Junction, Amazon and Ebay. The best way to incorporate these programs into your blog is to use advertisements or banners, or even reviews.

When you write a review, make sure to include an explanation of the product and its advantages, as well as the negatives (don't not include this information since mentioning negative aspects about the product can give your review credibility to readers) Also, describe what the product has done for you, and also include an associate link on the website that allows them to purchase the item.

This is a fantastic method as it allows you to pre-sell your customers and can help to boost your conversion rate.

Clickbank

http://www.clickbank.com

Clickbank sells digital products like ebooks, video courses and software. You will find a vast selection of products to market and it's easy to promote.

Additionally, many of payouts are between 65% and 75 percent and, on average, around $30. When you go to the Clickbank marketplace, you can filter the items by various types of criteria and categories.

Commission Junction

http://www.cj.com

Commission Junction has a range of affiliate programs for various products, both digital and physical. It is possible to earn commissions for a lead or sale.

Amazon

http://affiliate-program.amazon.com

While Amazon isn't paying as large of commissions as Clickbank or Commission Junction does, it can be effective in converting clicks into sales.

There are also a range of options they can offer to promote its products through your blog including rotating widgets that display a variety of merchandise and Amazon aStores which allow you to create a custom Amazon products store for your website.

Ebay

http://www.ebaypartnernetwork.com

Ebay is like Amazon and offers a wide selection of goods that you can advertise through your blog. They also offer an Click and Pay per Click program as well.

The Clickbank.com marketplace has hundreds of products you can advertise. It's easy to set up an account Clickbank.com Affiliate account which means you can begin looking into potential products and services right away.

Here's a brief outline of the best way to select the most effective products to meet your specific needs:

Visit http://www.ClickBank.com and click on the Marketplace link. Enter in the keywords that relate to your market for the purpose of creating an online page that lists items and services you could promote by becoming an affiliate of ClickBank affiliate.

If you go through the information of an offer you'll see statistics beneath each listing. One of them is known as gravity.

The gravity rating on Clickbank.com is an estimation from the latest sales of the product. Higher the gravity score higher, the more popular the product is for affiliates as it indicates to be getting a substantial quantity of sales.

If a product is also rated with a an extremely high gravity rating since sales are taken into consideration this means it's performing. This is the primary factor to consider when choosing a product to promote through Clickbank.com. It is essential to make sure that the product that you're advertising actually converts.

Google AdSense Ads

This is a kind of advertising that includes full-text classified ads being posted on your website or blogs.

When you apply to the program and get accepted, Google will display relevant AdSense advertisements on your site.

What happens is that each whenever a user of your website clicks on one of the Google ads that are displayed within your site, you be paid a small percentage. The typical cost per click amounts to approximately 20 cents, however it depends on how popular the keywords that are used in the advertisements are. Advertisers must spend more money to get more relevant keywords.

They are typically the key words for subjects that are highly profitable, like making money online, insuring credit cards, insurance, and so on. Keywords with higher competition can cost you up to $30 per click in some cases.

With AdSense you get paid for each click to ads displayed on your blog. It's free to sign up as an AdSense advertiser. You can create code which you copy and paste onto your blog's pages. These pages include advertising boxes from a variety of retailers.

Conclusion

WordPress has been around for a while and is constantly getting better and getting better. What was once an insignificant contribution to a blog platform has evolved into an incredible CMS which is ready to handle a website. If you learn some information concerning WordPress and the things it is able to accomplish, you'll likely think that it's a perfect option for your requirements.

WordPress users are beginning to realize that there's tremendous potential with an affordable starter theme such as Hello Theme and a free page builder such as Elementor. You can design your site quickly and efficiently, without spending a lot amount of time and effort in programming. The plugin and theme combination is in line with accordance with Open Source that figured out the best way to create WordPress the most popular CMS in the world.

E

CPSIA information can be obtained
at www.ICGtesting.com
Printed in the USA
BVHW050810140223
658473BV00009B/281